AMERICA'S ENTRY INTO WORLD WAR I

AMERICA'S ENTRY INTO WORLD WAR I

Submarines, Sentiment, or Security?

Edited by **HERBERT J. BASS**
Rutgers University

DRYDEN PRESS
HINSDALE, ILLINOIS

CONTENTS

The Challenge

—From *The Evening Sun, New York.*

UNCLE SAM: " You'll have to start it, William! "

INTRODUCTION

The outpouring of scholarly studies, popular histories, and magazine articles on World War I attests to a reawakened interest in that conflict. And with good reason, for World War I was an event of epochal importance in American and world history. From today's vantage point it is clear that the momentous events of the last fifty years followed as an almost direct consequence of the Great War.

Naturally enough, Americans have sought to learn the reasons for their nation's involvement in a conflict of such enormous consequence. The quest for causes is made more intriguing by the contrast of our action of 1917 with our attitude of 1914. When general warfare broke out in Europe, Americans were profoundly shocked, but almost all reacted with but a single thought: the war is none of our affair. President Wilson voiced the views of most Americans when he expressed the belief that the war was one "which cannot touch us." Yet less than three years later the United States was in it. What had happened in the intervening months to alter our position so completely? Why did the United States become involved in a war that Wilson himself had earlier described as one "with which we have nothing to do?"

The Wilsonian answer was that the war had been thrust upon us. Germany's declaration of unrestricted submarine warfare, constituting a repudiation of earlier pledges and an intolerable challenge to our rights and honor as a nation, left us no choice but to sever relations; the wanton acts of destruction which followed left us no choice but to resist. Although this was not a wholly satisfying answer to all Americans during the years of disillusionment that followed the war, the relationship between Germany's submarines and the involvement of the United States as simple, direct cause and effect prevailed as the orthodox view. Indeed, the first systematic history of America's intervention by a professional historian, Charles Seymour's *American Diplomacy during the World War* (1934), lent support to this interpretation. While not overlooking the country's traditional attachments to the Allies, Seymour concluded that the major cause of its entry was Germany's use of submarines.

1

His position, elaborated in the essay that opens this volume of readings, can perhaps best be expressed in his own question: If the German government had not resorted to unrestricted submarine warfare, would the United States have entered the war? While Seymour and other proponents of the submarine thesis concede the impossibility of a categorical answer to this hypothetical question, it is clear that, for them, to ask the question is to answer it.

For others this did not get to the heart of the matter. The implied answer to Seymour's question is, they concede, correct; it is the question itself that is wrong, for it can yield only the proximate cause of American intervention and not the fundamental, underlying one. To get at this one must press further and ask, Why did the German government decide to launch the unrestricted submarine campaign? The next group of readings addresses this question. The five selections differ in detail and emphasis but share one broad conclusion: the sentiment, policies, and overt behavior of the United States were so unneutral and prejudicial to Germany that the Imperial Government was left no choice but to play its final card. The writers, known as Revisionists, operated on the assumptions that our entry into war was an avoidable mistake and that the blame for it can be fixed on Americans.

The essay by Harry Elmer Barnes is the classic statement of American Revisionism. Rejecting Seymour's submarine thesis, Barnes finds the cause of American involvement in other factors: in Wilson's Anglo-Saxon background and intellectual outlook, in the intensely pro-Allied sympathies of Wilson's advisers, in an unneutral diplomacy that acquiesced in British violations of international law while it condemned less flagrant German violations, in the impact of British propaganda on American private and official opinion, in our extensive trade with the Allies, and in our financing of that trade with private loans. Here were the real reasons we entered the war, writes Barnes, although "there was no clear legal or moral basis for our so doing."

The next three selections, by Edwin Borchard, H. C. Peterson, and Charles Callan Tansill, each pick up and develop more fully one of the arguments sketched by Barnes. Borchard finds the cause of America's entry in our government's failure to follow long-established rules of neutrality. He believes the unneutral sentiment of Wilson, Secretary of State Lansing, Ambassador Page, and the President's peripatetic adviser, Colonel House, was before long translated into unneutral behavior. A life-long student of international law, Borchard builds his case on legal ground. Was there any basis in international law for Wilson's claim that armed belligerent merchantmen carrying Americans must be warned by submarine commanders before attack, even though the submarine was thus exposed to destruction by ramming or gunfire? Was not the administration spoiling for trouble in blocking the Gore-McLemore resolution in Congress which would have at least required a warning that Americans traveling on belligerent ships did so at their own risk? Did not a comparison of our stern submarine notes to Germany and our feeble protests to Britain over the illegal blockade, mail seizures from American ships, and the blacklisting of American firms offer evidence of our favoritism? Plainly, in Borchard's view, "we were unneutral, and we paid the price."

While Borchard aimed at proving that the United States did eschew true neutrality, Peterson sought to explain why we did so. His answer is that American neutrality and eventual entry into the war was primarily attributable to the success of British propaganda. Through its impact on American journalists, preachers, teachers, politicians, and other molders of opinion, British propaganda succeeded in producing an attitude of mind that identified England as the champion of democracy and civilization, Germany as their destroyer. This attitude in turn conditioned our government to pursue and our people to condone the unneutral policies that ultimately led to war.

The economic argument is developed in the selection by Tansill. Professedly a multicausationist, Tansill gives heavy stress in his *America Goes to War* to the close economic ties that developed between the Allies and American manufacturers and financiers. Drawing heavily on the investigations of the Special Senate Committee to Investigate the Munitions Industry—the famous Nye Committee of the mid-1930s—Tansill points to the increasingly bitter reaction of Germans to our supplying munitions to the Allies and financing the trade through bankers' loans. Even as German ire rose, he writes, those who profited from these economic ties were persuading the President through their influence on his key advisers to make the unneutral decisions that led to war.

In the final selection of this group Paul Birdsall develops the economic argument in a different form. Although Birdsall is not himself a Revisionist, in that he does not share the Revisionists' assumption about the avoidability of the war, his view of causation has become an important part of the Revisionist version of why the United States entered the war. Rejecting the simplistic view of both the Nye Committee and Tansill, Birdsall finds the government's decision permitting loans to have resulted not from the influence of profit-mongering munitions makers and bankers but rather from the need to maintain a domestic prosperity already dependent upon the war trade. As our prosperity became ever more intertwined with Allied trade, he explains, we were less and less able to stand firm against Allied encroachments on our neutral rights: the very measures of economic retaliation that might have brought Britain to heel would also have damaged our economy. In the eyes of the German military leaders we had become virtual allies of England. "The United States," concluded Hindenburg and Ludendorff, "could scarcely engage in more hostile activities than she has done up to this time." Thus the only argument that had restrained a full-scale submarine campaign

—that it would draw the United States into the war—lost its force, and the fateful submarine decision was made.

Taken together, Revisionist writings raise serious questions for the student to ponder: Did the United States fail to adhere to its neutral obligations? If we had adhered to them, could we have avoided involvement? Did British propaganda lead the American public and government down the path to war? How instrumental were economic factors in our involvement? Did munitions makers and bankers exert an undue influence on government officials? Were our diplomats and policy makers amateurish bunglers taken in by English professionals and hardheaded American financiers? Worse still, were they near-conspirators, men so determined that the Allies not be defeated that they manipulated American policy and sentiment to that end? Did the United States become involved, in short, because of folly, or knavery, or both? Or as Birdsall disturbingly suggests, was our involvement almost predetermined by impersonal domestic economic and political imperatives?

The Revisionists' approach and conclusions about causation were largely conditioned by the period in which they wrote and by their assumption that entry of the United States into World War I was an avoidable mistake, an unrelieved disaster for the nation and the world. Most Revisionist writing was done during the 1930s, less than two decades after World War I. Passions still ran high, perspective was short, and important source material remained generally unavailable. Then too, the 1930s were a decade in which disillusionment with World War I, antipathy to bankers and big businessmen, the Great Depression, and a resurgent isolationism all converged to influence not only the general public but the scholarly community as well.

The 1940s and 1950s brought a challenge to the Revisionist assumptions about our entry into World War I. Dispassion replaced passion, a lengthened perspective nurtured new viewpoints, and important new sources, such as the Wilson papers, became available for scholars' examination. But perhaps most important, American participation in World War II against Nazi Germany inevitably led to a review of these assumptions. Was the cause of our intervention rooted almost solely in domestic factors and decisions after all, or might it be found in factors over which the United States had little or no control? Could the United States really have avoided involvement at no serious cost to its interest and honor? Was it, after all, a mistake for the United States to have entered the European war? Was the outcome really of insufficient concern to the United States to justify its intervention?

In dealing with these questions, some postwar historians have sharply taken issue with the Revisionist assertion that the unleashing of the submarine was primarily a response to unneutral acts of the United States. The selection by Edward H. Buehrig, for example, critically examines the view that the primary cause of America's entry was economic. Buehrig grants that

German resentment over the country's munitions trade was real, but he questions whether it was the controlling factor in Germany's actions. Even had we shipped no arms at all, he asks, could the series of circumstances that led to the submarine impasse have been avoided? As for the alleged influence of bankers on government officials, Buehrig points to the lack of any concrete evidence that administration officials actually responded to any banker pressure to assure the collectibility of their loans by intervening. He concludes that not merely a denial of trade and loans to the Allies but a granting of such trade and loans to Germany would have been required to forestall the German military's decision to launch the submarine campaign in 1917.

In the next selection another recent student, Ernest R. May, denies that unrestricted submarine warfare was a simplistic reaction to American policies. Basing his arguments on examination of German sources, May concludes that the German decision was chiefly conditioned by various pressures within Germany itself—pressures from the navalists, annexationists, the political Right, army leaders, portions of the press, and finally from much of the public itself, wearying of the inconclusive struggle and demanding the fullest use of a weapon that many believed could bring the war to a speedy end. By January 1917 Chancellor Bethmann-Hollweg could no longer resist these pressures, and the fateful decision was made—with little reference, argues May, to the question of America's policies on loans, trade, interpretations of international law, or unneutral sentiment in high places. May's conclusion puts him in essential agreement with Charles Seymour. Though he sees the problem of causation as a more complex one than Seymour does, and though he travels a substantially different route of inquiry, in the final analysis the submarine was, in his view as in Seymour's, the primary cause of American involvement.

The final selection of this group is by Arthur S. Link, whose position is close to those of Seymour and May. In Link's view Wilson and the United States government conscientiously pursued a neutral course, and never more so than during the critical months from the *Sussex* episode in spring 1916 to the announcement on January 31, 1917, of the German decision to resort to unrestricted submarine warfare. He argues that that decision resulted from the German High Command's optimistic assessment of the military situation and its belief that a quick, clear-cut victory lay within its grasp through the unlimited use of submarines.

Thus, although neither Buehrig, May, nor Link deny the legitimacy of the Revisionists' question—Why did the German government decide to launch the unrestricted submarine campaign?—as an approach to determining the cause of America's entry, they have vigorously denied the validity of the Revisionists' answer. Moreover, to establish their point more conclusively, they have added a question of their own: Even if the United States had interpreted its neutral obligations differently, would the Germans, short of achieving a *de facto* alliance with the United States, have foregone the fullest use of a weapon which by 1917 seemed to most of them to hold the promise of quick victory? And if not, what choice would the United States have had but to respond to such a challenge?

And what of the earlier assumption that American intervention had been a colossal mistake: that the outcome of the European conflict was of no great concern to the United States, that even a German victory would have been preferable to American involvement? Not only did this assumption evaporate with the outbreak of World War II; its very opposite was asserted by some to have been a primary cause of American intervention. Writing in the spring of 1941 at the height of the Nazi peril, the political analyst Walter Lippmann offered the view that it was precisely because the United States did have a stake in the outcome of World War I that it entered the conflict. Recognizing that a successful submarine campaign would disrupt the European power balance and result in the passing of control of the Atlantic from Britain to Germany, and that such an outcome would jeopardize American security, the United States intervened.

The thesis that the Wilson administration took the United States into war in order to protect its security soon became a focal point of scholarly inquiry and debate, represented in the last group of readings. More than a decade after Lippmann wrote the article that opens this section, his interpretation received impressive support in Buehrig's *Woodrow Wilson and the Balance of Power* (1955), from which a selection appears in the preceding group of readings. But other students of World War I have rejected the security thesis as unsubstantiated by historical fact. Among them are a number of scholars, represented here by George F. Kennan and Robert E. Osgood, who did so with the greatest of reluctance, for this interpretation was a specially fetching one for them. These are the writers of the so-called "Realist" school, who decry a moralistic and legalistic approach to foreign policy and argue instead for a "realistic" understanding of national self-interest and "realistic" policies to promote it. Far from recoiling, as would the Revisionists, from the frankly interventionist, security-oriented policy that Lippmann advocates, the Realists welcome and encourage it as a wholly desirable and realistic approach to American foreign policy. They agree with Lippmann that if the United States had to enter the war, the most eminently proper grounds for such intervention was the maintenance of its security.

But was this in fact the reason for our entry? The selections by Kennan and Osgood breathe a wistful "would that it were so," but finally conclude that it did not happen that way. Kennan's essay sets forth the essentials of the Realist position: the government and people of the United States had no real understanding of the causes and objects of the European war; they failed to recognize a stake in its outcome; an intervention to preserve a European power balance that had historically served our security interests well would have been realistic and wise; we entered instead over an inflated issue of neutral rights. Kennan's conclusion is that we entered the right war for the wrong reasons.

While Kennan establishes the general ground of the Realist school, Osgood addresses his study directly to the Lippmann thesis. If that thesis is correct, writes Osgood, should not one expect to find evidence that President Wilson and the American public recognized that a tipping of the European power balance in Germany's favor posed a threat to American security? But an investigation yields no such evidence, he reports; instead, he finds that Wilson specifically rejected balance-of-power considerations and that the American public saw almost no connection between the European war and the physical security of the United States. Both Osgood and Kennan conclude that the United States actually intervened for misguided, sentimental reasons: for neutral rights, for national honor, and for a vague ideal of service to humanity, all of which became identified with the submarine issue. Was not sentiment, then, rather than security the cause of America's intervention? Ironically, although both Revisionists and Realists agree on this, their conclusions differ radically. Revisionists assert that it was an unneutral sentiment that led to unneutral policies resulting in the country's entry; Realists insist that, on the contrary, a sentiment unrealistically attached to the defense of neutral rights led us into war.

Was it, then, German use of the submarine that was the fundamental cause of American intervention in World War I? Or is the real cause to be found in the country's unneutral sentiment, policies, and actions, to which Germany made the only response it could conceive? Did the American government and people discern a threat to our security, to Anglo-American control of the Atlantic sea lanes, or to the maintenance of a favorable power balance in Europe, and intervene for any of these reasons? Or was American intervention the result of an unrealistic, misguided sentimentalism? For our generation even more than for an earlier one, these questions are of greater than passing interest. For it is with the perspective of our generation that the significance of World War I is more clearly visible, not only as an occurence of major import in the evolution of the United States toward larger world responsibilities, but also as an event which set in motion developments that continue to shape, and shake, our world.

A professor of history for a quarter century at Yale University and then its president, CHARLES SEYMOUR (1885–1963) was long the dean of Wilson scholars. An earlier study of the diplomatic background of the war and the editing of the papers of Colonel House qualified him to write the first scholarly narrative of American diplomacy in World War I. In that and subsequent works Seymour argued the view that the German submarine was the cause of America's entry into the war. In the essay below Seymour, replying to Revisionist attacks on the submarine thesis, concludes that Wilson was driven from a long-maintained position of neutrality by the only thing that could have done so—unrestricted submarine warfare.*

The Submarine and American Intervention

. . . There was at least one American who was acutely aware of why the United States was brought into the World War. This was the President of the United States, who for nearly three years struggled to maintain neutrality in the face of difficulties that finally proved uncontrollable. Whether as a basis for future policy, or merely to set the historical record straight, it is worth while to review Woodrow Wilson's fight to avoid intervention.

Any inquiry into the causes of American participation in the war must begin with the personality of Wilson. His office conferred upon him a determining influence in foreign policy which was heightened by the troubled state of affairs abroad. His character was such that he never let this influence slip into other hands. He was his own foreign secretary. Conscious of the power and character of public opinion, "under bonds," as he put it, to public sentiment, he nevertheless made the major decisions on his own responsibility. He delivered his "too proud to fight" speech and he sent Bernstorff home without stopping to ask what the man in the street would say. Dominant sentiment in the United States was certainly pro-Ally. American economic prosperity, furthermore, depended upon the maintenance of our trade with the Allies. But it is a far cry from these facts to

* "American Neutrality: The Experience of 1914–17," by Charles Seymour. Reprinted by special permission from *Foreign Affairs*, October 1935. Copyright by the Council on Foreign Relations Inc., New York.

the assumption that because of them we adopted a policy that pointed toward intervention. It would be necessary to show that emotional sympathy and material interests overcame the strong pacifistic sentiment of Congress and people. It would especially be necessary to show that because of them Wilson first adopted a discriminatory attitude toward Germany and then surrendered his determination to keep the country out of war.

Ample evidence is now available regarding Wilson's sentiments toward the belligerents. If it reveals an underlying personal sympathy with the Allies, it also reveals a studied insistence not to permit that feeling to affect national policy. He was so far successful that he was attacked in turn by each belligerent group as being favorable to the other. There can be no question that he regarded the maintenance of peace as his first duty. Always he held to the double principle he formulated at the moment he was smarting under the news of the *Arabic*'s sinking in August, 1915: "1. The people of this country count on me to keep them out of the war; 2. It would be a calamity to the world at large if we should be actively drawn into the conflict and so deprived of all disinterested influence over the settlement." He maintained this attitude in the face of what he regarded as gross affronts by Germany. "The country is undoubtedly back of me in the whole matter," he wrote privately in September, 1915, "and I feel myself under bonds to it to show patience to the utmost. My chief puzzle is to determine where patience ceases to be a virtue."

But across the determination to preserve peace ran the equally strong determination to preserve the neutral rights of the country. There was a higher principle which the President placed above peace: the honor of the United States. The outcome of this contradiction would be determined not by Wilson's policy but by that of the belligerents. He said in January, 1916:

I know that you are depending upon me to keep this Nation out of the war. So far I have done so and I pledge you my word that, God helping me, I will—if it is possible. But you have laid another duty upon me. You have bidden me see to it that nothing stains or impairs the honor of the United States, and that is a matter not within my control; that depends upon what others do, not upon what the Government of the United States does. Therefore there may at any moment come a time when I cannot preserve both the honor and the peace of the United States. Do not exact of me an impossible and contradictory thing.

Against both groups of belligerents Wilson steadily maintained American neutral rights. It is by no means a fact that he accepted British and Allied infractions of what he described as "hitherto fixed international law." The notes of protest which he sponsored and which so greatly annoyed those who, like Ambassador Page, frankly favored the Allied cause, made clear that the United States did not, and would not, recognize the legality of the Allied pseudo-blockade. In the late summer of 1916 the President secured from Congress wide powers permitting him to prohibit loans and to impose embargoes if retaliatory measures appeared advisable. A few weeks later he asked House to warn Sir Edward Grey "in the strongest terms" that the American people were "growing more and more impatient with the intolerable conditions of neutrality, their feeling as hot against Great Britain as it was first against Germany. . . ."

That he did not actually exercise the pressure of embargoes against the British and French resulted from two factors. The first was that the conflict over Allied interference with neutral trade was pushed into the background at critical moments by the more immediate and intense conflict with Germany over the submarine campaign. "If Germany had not alienated American sympathies," wrote Colonel House, "by her mode of warfare, the United States would not have put up with Allied control of American trade on the high seas." The fact has been emphasized by Winston Churchill. "The first German U-boat campaign," he writes, "gave us our greatest assistance. It altered the whole position of our controversies with America. A great relief became immediately apparent."

The second reason for not pushing the diplomatic conflict with the Allies to the point of retaliatory measures lay in the economic interests of America. Any practicable measures designed to enforce our interpretation of international law would have ruined the interests they meant to safeguard. By our formal protests we protected our ultimate property rights and built up a case for future damages to be proved before an international tribunal. Through private negotiations we secured in large measure the protection of immediate commercial interests. Whatever the inconvenience and delays experienced in our trade with the northern European neutrals, American foreign commerce was deriving rich profits. Allied command of the sea did not touch our pockets so much as our pride. As Ambassador Spring Rice cabled to Grey, it seemed "objectionable not because it is what it is, but because it is so all-pervading." Thus, if Wilson had destroyed

the basis of our prosperity in order to compel immediate acceptance of the American interpretation of international law, which very few Americans understood and which even now is not entirely clear, he would have provoked something like a revolt against his administration. "If it came to the last analysis," wrote House to Wilson in the summer of 1915, "and we placed an embargo upon munitions of war and foodstuffs to please the cotton men, our whole industrial and agricultural machinery would cry out against it." Wilson's policy was designed not to favor the Allies but to protect the immediate interests of the nation and at the same time to preserve our ultimate legal rights. He yielded no principle and surrendered no claim.

The German attack upon American rights Wilson believed to be of an entirely different nature and one that must be met by different methods. The intensive submarine campaign was the answer to the system of Allied maritime control; logically, an excuse might be found for it. But its effects upon neutral rights were far more disastrous. For technical reasons and to operate effectively, the submarines must make their attack without warning, destroy blindly, escape as speedily as possible, leaving the sinking merchant ship, which might be neutral or belligerent, which might or might not carry contraband, with no assurance of what would happen to passengers and crew. To Wilson and to dominant American opinion, such wholesale methods of destroying enemy and neutral commerce were shocking. This was no question of "juridical niceties." The submarine campaign, unlike the Allied blockade, involved undiscriminating destruction of American property rights. It permitted no distinction between contraband and free goods. The Allied system gave to the American shipper reasonable assurance of safe passage after he had complied with certain formalities. Under the threat of the submarine the shipper faced the risk of losing his entire cargo. The Allied system did not involve the loss of American ships; if held in a British prize court the owner could find protection for them in legal procedure. The German submarine threatened the loss of the ship and the death of the crew and passengers as well.

Thus, from the point of view of material interests, there could be no comparison between the damage resulting to Americans from the Allied blockade and that from the intensive submarine campaign. If the latter were permitted, under protests comparable to those sent to the Allies, the result would be an almost complete blockade of American commerce, since shippers would not dare send cargoes and crew out to destruction. A clear illustration of the effect of the submarine campaign on American commercial, industrial, and agricultural interests was given by the congestion of our ports that followed the threat of submarine attacks in February and March, 1917. Freights were snarled, goods were spoiled, business was menaced with a complete tie-up.

Even so, Wilson might not have taken his firm stand against the submarine if merely property rights had been threatened. He was always careful not to interpret national policy in terms of purely material interests. Despite the difficulties involved, the economic aspects of the diplomatic conflict with Germany might have been adjudicated. But the submarine warfare involved attacks upon American lives, whether sailors on merchant ships or passengers. To Wilson it

seemed a war on humanity. Between property interests and human rights there lay a clear distinction. It was brought home to all America when, on May 7, 1915, the *Lusitania* was sunk without warning, over eleven hundred persons drowned, men, women, and children, among them more than one hundred and twenty Americans. Wilson wrote:

The sinking of passenger ships involves principles of humanity which throw into the background any special circumstances of detail that may be thought to affect the cases, principles which lift it, as the Imperial German Government will no doubt be quick to recognize and acknowledge, out of the class of ordinary subjects of diplomatic discussion or of international controversy. . . . The Government of the United States is contending for something much greater than mere rights of property or privileges of commerce. It is contending for nothing less high and sacred than the rights of humanity, which every Government honors itself in respecting and no Government is justified in resigning on behalf of those under its care and authority.

It has been frequently suggested that since the submarine campaign was designed to interrupt the flow of munitions from the United States to the Allies, Wilson might have imposed embargoes upon the export of munitions as a diplomatic bribe to Germany to give up the intensive use of the submarine. There is no indication that the President ever seriously considered this course. He was willing to utilize embargoes, if necessary as measures of retaliation against the Allies in the defense of American rights. But he was not willing to penalize ourselves in order to redress the inherent disadvantage of Germany resulting from Allied command of the seas. He agreed with Lansing that such a policy ran counter to the neutral duties of the United States. It would certainly have ruined not merely the "war babies" of industry, but the cotton and wheat growers, the copper producers, the iron and steel workers, and have thrown the country back into the bleak depression and unemployment from which it had just emerged.

There is no evidence that even the broadest sort of American embargo would have induced the Germans to forego the intensive use of the submarine. They meant to stop British imports of all raw materials, especially foodstuffs, not merely from the United States but from South America, India, and the Dominions. The purpose of the submarine campaign was far wider than the interruption of the Allied "munitions" trade with America; it was, according to the testimony given to the Reichstag investigating committee, designed to throw over the British the deadly fear of complete starvation and thus to compel them to sue for peace on German terms. Hindenburg and Ludendorff made quite plain that, in the winter of 1916–17, nothing but the prospect of immediate peace on such terms could have prevented the resumption of the submarine campaign.

Wilson, of course, might have avoided a break with Germany by surrendering the right to send American ships and citizens out on the high seas. Thus they would not be sunk by submarines. Such a policy was suggested by Mr. Bryan and was later embodied in the Gore-McLemore resolutions brought before Congress. The President believed that no government was justified in making this surrender. Through his protests to the Allies he had secured, without yielding any principle, a working arrangement that gave reasonable protection to American commercial interests. Now if, under the threat of the German submarine, he withdrew protection on the seas from American goods, sailors, and passengers, he would sacrifice interests that no protests could compensate and yield principles that nothing in the future could make good. He wrote to Senator Stone:

No nation, no group of nations, has the right, while war is in progress, to alter or disregard the principles which all nations have agreed upon in mitigation of the horrors and sufferings of war; and if the clear rights of American citizens should ever unhappily be abridged or denied by such action, we should, it seems to me, have in honor no choice as to what our own course should be. . . . We covet peace and shall preserve it at any cost but the loss of honor. To forbid our people to exercise their rights for fear we might be called upon to vindicate them would be a deep humiliation indeed.

It was all very well, Wilson pointed out, to argue that the material value of these rights could not be compared with the cost of a war. But if you begin to surrender accepted rights, where do you stop?

If in this instance we allowed expediency to take the place of principle, the door would inevitably be opened to still further concessions. Once accept a single abatement of right, and many other humiliations would certainly follow. . . . What we are contending for in this matter is of the very essence of the things that have made America a sovereign nation. She cannot yield them without conceding her own impotency as a Nation and making virtual surrender of her independent position among the nations of the world.

Such was Wilson's position, written for all the world and especially for Germany to read. He maintained it consistently from the first declaration of submarine warfare in February, 1915, two years before the final break, when he warned the German Government that it would be held to "a strict accountability" for acts endangering American lives and property, and that the American Government would take any necessary steps to "secure to American citizens the full enjoyment of their acknowledged rights on the high seas." This warning was translated into specific terms a year later, after the sinking of the *Sussex*, taking the form of an ultimatum which left no further room for negotiation:

Unless the Imperial Government should now immediately declare and effect an abandonment of its present methods of submarine warfare against passenger and freight-carrying vessels, the Government of the United States can have no choice but to sever diplomatic relations with the German Empire altogether.

The Germans yielded, if only for the moment, as a result of this definite warning. During the course of 1915 they had taken Von Bernstorff's warnings not too seriously, and heeded them largely because they had not yet themselves realized what a powerful weapon they possessed in the submarine. After Wilson's *Sussex* note they were under no illusions. "There was no longer any doubt in Berlin," wrote the German Ambassador, "that persistence in the point of view they had hitherto adopted would bring about a break with the United States." But in the early autumn Hindenburg and Ludendorff threw their influence in favor of a resumption of the submarine campaign. The discussions in Berlin were clearly based upon the assumption of war with the United States. Bethmann-Hollweg later testified before the Reichstag committee:

The U-boat war meant a break and, later, war with America. It was on this point that for years the argument between the military and the political branch had turned. The decisive point was that the Supreme High Command of the Army from now on was absolutely determined to assume the responsibility of the risk which an American war meant. . . .

The one chance of preventing the resumption of the submarine campaign, and thus keeping the United States out of war, lay in peace negotiations. Bernstorff judged correctly that neither Wilson nor public opinion would permit America to enter the war on any issue other than the submarine, and that it was vital to secure a postponement of the intensive campaign. He telegraphed to von Jagow, July 13, 1916:

If it once comes to peace negotiations between the combatants, I regard it as out of the question—even were they to fail—that the United States would enter the war against us. American public feeling in favor of peace is too strong for that. It required the hysterical excitement roused by the *Lusitania* question, and the incidents connected with it, to produce a state of mind among Americans which at times made war seem inevitable. In the absence of similar incidents, such a state of feeling could not be aroused.

Hence the eagerness with which he pressed upon Colonel House the importance of peace action by Wilson before it was too late. Hence also the determination with which Wilson, who realized the approaching danger, prepared his peace note of December 18, 1916. He wanted to make it, he wrote House, "the strongest and most convincing thing I ever penned."

In the circumstances the effort was bound to fail. Its effect was confused by the issuance of Bethmann's peace statement on December 12, which made Wilson's note appear to the Allies as part of a plan to rescue the Central Powers from defeat. The Allies were quite unwilling to negotiate with an unbeaten Germany. The Germans were determined to insist upon terms which the Allies would not have accepted until all hope of victory had faded. Neither side wished the mediation of Wilson. The British, according to Sir William Wiseman, felt that Wilson merely talked about ideals for which the Allies were dying. "We entertain but little hope," von Jagow had written to Bernstorff, "for the result of the exercise of good offices by one whose instincts are all in favor of the English point of view, and who in addition to this, is so naïve a statesman as President Wilson." The new German Foreign Secretary, Zimmermann, said to the budget committee of the Reichstag: "The good thing about the break with the United States is that we have finally gotten rid of this person as peace mediator."

Wilson was not discouraged by the failure of the December peace notes. He worked all through January to secure a private statement of German terms, equipped with which he could start negotiations with the Allies. He was determined to save American neutrality. On January 4, 1917, in reply to House's suggestion of the need of military preparation "in the event of war," the President insisted: "There will be no war. This country does not intend to become involved in this war. We are the only one of the great white nations that is free from war today, and it would be a crime against civilization for us to go in." On January 22 he delivered before the Senate the address which he hoped would serve as a general basis for a negotiated peace, a settlement that would leave neither the one side nor the other crushed and revengeful, "a peace without victory." It opened, as British writers later insisted, the "last opportunity of ending the war with a real peace. For America was still pacific and impartial. . . . But unhappily for mankind, the British and Prussian war machines had by then taken charge."

It is possible that if Germany had then held her hand Wilson might have been able to force negotiations. The Allies were begining to scrape the bottom of the money chest and the time was approaching when they would be dependent upon American credits. He could soon have exercised strong pressure upon them. On the other side the Kaiser, Bethmann, and Bernstorff had no profound confidence in the submarine and were inclined toward compromise. But the decision had already been taken in Germany. On January 9 Hindenburg and Holtzendorf insisted that all chance of peace had disappeared and forced approval of the intensive submarine campaign. On January 31 Bernstorff gave notice that from the following day the engagements of the pledge given after the sinking of the *Sussex* would no longer be observed.

Thus ended Wilson's last efforts to achieve a compromise peace, and the rupture between Germany and the United States became inevitable. The President saw no escape from the fulfilment of the warning he had given the previous April. The shock was the worse for Wilson inasmuch as it came just as he hoped to initiate mediation. He said "he felt as if the world had suddenly reversed itself; that after going from east to west, it had begun to go from west to east and he could not get his balance." Resentment against Germany, with whom he had been working for peace, was strong. He felt with House that Germany "desires some justification for her submarine warfare and thought she could get it by declaring her willingness to make peace." Bernstorff himself insists that it was the German declaration of submarine warfare and nothing else that mattered with Wilson.

From that time henceforward—there can be no question of any earlier period, because up to that time he had been in constant negotiation with us—he regarded the Imperial Government as morally condemned. . . . After January 31, 1917, Wilson himself was a different man. Our rejection of his proposal to mediate, by our announcement of the unrestricted U-boat war, which was to him utterly incomprehensible, turned him into an embittered enemy of the Imperial Government.

Even after the diplomatic rupture Wilson waited long weeks, to give every opportunity to the Germans to avoid war. Only actual overt acts would persuade him that they would carry their policy into effect. He was willing to negotiate everything except the sinking of passenger and merchant ships without warning. The Germans showed no sign of weakening. When it was suggested that America might be kept neutral if the submarines "overlooked" American boats, the Kaiser wrote on the margin of the memorandum which disapproved the suggestion on technical grounds: "Agreed, reject. . . . Now, once for all, an *end* to negotiations with America. If Wilson wants war, let him make it, and let him then have it." On March 27, following the sinking of four American ships, the President took the decision, and on April 2 he asked Congress to declare the existence of a state of war with Germany.

So far as tests can be applied, Wilson's position was approved by the American people. Like him they were determined to stay at peace so far as the exercise of their acknowledged rights could keep them at peace, but they regarded the submarine attacks as acts of war. They were by no means prepared to sacrifice American rights on the seas and adopt a policy of nonintercourse with European belligerents and neutrals which would have resulted in economic depression or disaster in the United States. So much is indicated by the votes in Congress on the Gore-McLemore resolutions and the armed shipping bill which gave overwhelming endorsement to Wilson's policy. On the other hand, whatever the emotional sympathy for the Allied cause in the United States and however close Allied and American commercial interests, the prevailing sentiment of the people was indelibly for peace until the submarines sank American ships. They rewarded the patience with which Wilson carried on long negotiations over the *Lusitania* as well as the firmness with which he issued the *Sussex* ultimatum by reëlecting him President in the autumn of 1916. He owed his victory to the pacifists. So far from being accused of chauvinism because of the stand he had taken against the submarine campaign, he was presented and elected on the basis of having "kept us out of war." But when on April 2, following the destruction of American ships, he declared that peace was no longer consistent with honor, Congress voted for war by tremendous majorities.

It frequently happens that the occasion for an event is mistaken for its cause. Sometimes, however, the occasion and the cause are the same. There is every evidence that the sole factor that could have driven Wilson from neutrality in the spring of 1917 was the resumption of the submarine campaign. . . .

One could scarcely find an essay more at variance with Seymour's views in its assumptions, approach, and conclusions than this piece by HARRY ELMER BARNES (1889–   ). Embattled knight of American Revisionism, Barnes is representative of those liberals whose disillusionment with the war was complete. His *Genesis of the World War* (1926) contained one of the earliest statements of Revisionism. The selection below is drawn from a 1940 essay which Barnes regards as his "final testament" on World War I. It is, for the sheer breadth of its attack, one of the best examples of Revisionist writing, embracing in one form or another nearly every thesis elaborated upon by later writers of this school.*

▶ # The Submarine Thesis Challenged: The Broad Revisionist Statement

The United States could not have been more perfectly set up for neutrality than it was in July and August, 1914. President Woodrow Wilson was a lifelong and deeply conscientious pacifist. His convictions in this matter were not emotional or impressionistic, but had been based upon deep study and prolonged reflection. Moreover, he was married to a woman noted for pacific sentiments and firm convictions on such matters. She strongly backed up her husband in his pacific beliefs and policies. As Secretary of State, we had in William Jennings Bryan the world's outstanding pacifist. His pacifism was notably courageous; he was willing to stick by his guns even in the face of malicious criticism.

Moreover, Wilson was almost uniquely well informed as to the essentials of the European situation before war broke out in the summer of 1914. He had sent his personal representative, Colonel Edward M. House, to Europe to study the international situation and to report to him upon it. Whatever his later mistakes, Colonel House sized up matters in Europe with almost perfect sagacity and understanding in May, 1914. He concluded his observations with the statement that "whenever England consents, France and Russia will close in on Germany."

If one were to summarize, as briefly as

* From Harry Elmer Barnes, "The World War of 1914–1918," in Willard Waller (ed.), *War in the Twentieth Century* (New York: Dryden Press, 1940), pp. 71–82. Reprinted without footnotes by permission of the author.

this, the outcome of the years of scholarly study since 1918, with respect to responsibility for the World War, a more perfect estimate and verdict than Colonel House's phrase could not be rendered in the same number of words. Further, the Colonel pointed out that, whatever the Kaiser's emotional shortcomings, he wished for European peace. On the other hand, he stated candidly that George V of England was "the most pugnacious monarch loose in these parts."

When war broke out, President Wilson's statements were a model of neutral procedure. He issued a formally correct neutrality proclamation and went on to exhort his countrymen to be neutral in thought as well as in action. There is no doubt that he was completely neutral at heart in August, 1914. Less than three years later, however, in April, 1917, he went before Congress and told its members that "God helping her," this country could do no other than make war on Germany. Moreover, he returned from the Capitol to the White House and made statements to his secretary, Joseph P. Tumulty, indicating that, at the time of his war message, he had so far changed his attitude that he could not believe he ever had been neutral. He cited with approval an article by the correspondent of the *Manchester Guardian* stating that Mr. Wilson had always been sympathetic with the Allies and had wished to throw this country into war on their side just as soon as circumstances would permit.

We shall first briefly consider some of the reasons why Wilson altered his point of view, since no other set of circumstances could alone have forced us into the war, if Wilson had not been favorable to our entry by the spring of 1917.

First and foremost, we must take into account the fact that Wilson's intellec-

tual perspective was predominantly Anglo-Saxon. He had little knowledge of, or sympathy with, continental European culture and institutions. His great intellectual heroes were such English writers as John Milton, John Locke, Adam Smith and Walter Bagehot. He did his graduate work in the Johns Hopkins University Seminar under Herbert Baxter Adams, where the "Anglo-Saxon Myth" reigned supreme. Wilson was a persistent student and admirer of the English constitution and frankly regarded the British system of government as superior to our own.

Then Wilson had in his cabinet and among his ambassadors men who were intensely pro-English or pro-Ally in their sympathies. Such were Secretaries Lindley M. Garrison and David F. Houston. Walter Hines Page, our ambassador in London, was even more intensely pro-English than Wilson. Indeed, he frequently went to such excesses as to annoy the President. When Bryan was succeeded by Robert Lansing, the most crucial post in the cabinet went to another vehemently pro-English sympathizer. The biases of Page and Lansing made it difficult to pursue forthright diplomacy with Great Britain.

Another major difficulty lay in the fact that President Wilson and Secretary Lansing did not formulate and execute a fair and consistent line of diplomatic procedure. They had one type of international law for England and the Allies, and quite another for Germany. They all but allowed Great Britain to run wild in the violation of international law and of our neutral rights, while they insisted on holding Germany "to strict accountability."

England started out in 1914 by making a scrap of paper out of the Declaration of London governing contraband in wartime. Next, we proceeded to allow her to make use of armed belligerent merchantmen as if they were peaceful commercial vessels. England violated our neutral rights far more extensively between 1914 and 1917 than she did before the War of 1812, even to the point of flying the American flag.

Wilson came to believe, however, that Great Britain was fighting for civilization and that so trivial a thing as international law must not be allowed to stand in her way. Wilson's Attorney-General, Thomas W. Gregory, tells of the rebuke which the President administered to certain cabinet members when they protested over the flagrant British violation of our neutral rights: "After patiently listening, Mr. Wilson said, in that quiet way of his, that the ordinary rules of conduct had no application to the situation; that the Allies were standing with their backs to the wall, fighting wild beasts; that he would permit nothing to be done l our country to hinder or embarrass them in the prosecution of the war unless admitted rights were grossly violated, and that this policy must be understood as settled." Bryan protested against our unfair and unneutral diplomacy and ultimately resigned because he could not square his conscience with it.

Secretary Lansing admits in his *Memoirs* that he made no real pretense of holding England to the tenets of international law. He tells us that after the sinking of the *Lusitania* he thought we should be fighting on the side of the Allies and that he was determined to do nothing which would prove embarrassing to us when we later took up our position as a military comrade of the Allied powers. He persisted in this attitude, even though he was honest enough to write after the war that in 1917 we had as good, if not better, legal grounds for fighting Britain as for fighting Germany.

Ambassador Page even went so far as to collaborate with Sir Edward Grey in answering the protests of his own government, an unparalleled procedure which, when revealed, outraged even so pro-Ally a journal as the *New York Times*.

We thus encouraged and perpetuated the illegally extensive British blockade, which provoked the German submarine warfare. In time, we made war on the latter, though it was our unneutral diplomacy which contributed, in large part, to the continuance of both the British blockade and the German submarine activities.

Wilson was deeply affected by the criticisms to which he was subjected by prominent Americans sympathetic with the Allies and in favor of intervention on their side. He was stung by the famous speeches of Theodore Roosevelt on "The Shadows of Shadow Lawn," and by the latter's reference to Wilson's diplomatic statements as examples of "weasel words." He was particularly annoyed by the statement of Elihu Root that "first he shakes his fist and then he shakes his finger."

On the other hand, Wilson was human enough to take note of the praise which was showered upon him by the press when he made a bellicose statement or led a preparedness parade. This contrasted sharply with the bitter criticism he evoked when he made a statesmanlike remark, such as that a country might be "too proud to fight," or that the only desirable peace would be "a peace without victory."

Wilson was also profoundly moved by the British propaganda relative to German atrocities and territorial ambitions.

This was particularly true after Lord Bryce lent his name to the prestige and veracity of the propaganda stories as to German savagery. Of all living Englishmen, Bryce was probably the man whom Wilson most admired and trusted. When Bryce sponsored the propaganda lies, Wilson came to believe that they must have a substantial basis in fact. This helped on his rationalization that England was fighting the battle of human civilization against wild beasts. . . .

When, as an outcome of these various influences, Wilson had been converted to intervention, he rationalized his change of attitude on the basis of a noble moral purpose. As he told Jane Addams in the spring of 1917, he felt that the United States must be represented at the peace conference which would end the World War if there was to be any hope of a just and constructive peace. But Wilson could be at the peace conference only if the United States had previously entered the World War.

It is still asserted by many writers, such as Professor Charles Seymour, that the resumption of submarine warfare by Germany was the sole reason for Wilson's determination to enter the war on the Allied side. But we know that he had been converted to intervention long before January, 1917. A year earlier, he had sent Colonel House to Europe with a plan to put us in the war on the side of the Allies if Germany would not accept peace terms obviously unfavorable to her. But even such peace terms for Germany were rejected by the British leaders, who felt sure of American aid anyway and were determined to crush Germany. Yet this British rebuff did not lead Wilson to lose heart in his efforts to put this country into the war.

His next step was taken in this country. Early in April, 1916, Wilson called into consultation Speaker Champ Clark of the House of Representatives and Congressional leaders Claude Kitchin and H. D. Flood, and sounded them out to see if they would support him in a plan to bring the United States into the war on the side of the Allies. This was the famous "Sunrise Conference" described later by Gilson Gardner in *McNaught's Monthly* of June, 1925. These men sharply refused to sanction any such policy, and Wilson allowed the campaign of 1916 to be fought out on the slogan, "He kept us out of war." Wilson did not dare to risk splitting the Democratic Party over entry into the war before the campaign of 1916 had successfully ended. The existence of the "Sunrise Conference" has been fully verified by Professor A. M. Arnett in his scholarly book on Claude Kitchin.

Wilson was convinced after the failure of the "Sunrise Conference" that there was no hope of getting the country into war until after the election. The sentiment of the nation was for peace. If he was elected as an exponent of peace and then went into war the country as a whole would believe that he had done his best to "keep us out of war." He would have a united country behind him. Hence, he and Colonel House sent Governor Martin Glynn of New York and Senator Ollie James of Kentucky to the Democratic National Convention at St. Louis, in June, 1916, with instructions to make keynote speeches emphasizing Wilson's heroic efforts to keep us out of war.

Thus was fashioned the famous slogan "He kept us out of war," which reelected Woodrow Wilson to the presidency almost a year after Colonel House, following Wilson's directions, had declared that: "The United States would like Great Britain to do whatever would help the United States to aid the Allies."

The campaign and election of 1916 were very really a referendum on war, and the people voted against war. This is illuminating as an illustration of the fallacy that a war referendum, such as the Ludlow Amendment, would, by itself alone, suffice to keep us out of war, but the election of 1916 does offer definite proof that Wilson was not pushed into war by popular demand.

The influence exerted by - American finance upon our entry into the World War has been revealed in Ray Stannard Baker's *Life and Letters of Woodrow Wilson,* in the volumes of the Nye armament investigation, and in Professor C. C. Tansill's *America Goes to War.*

At the outset, the international bankers were not by any means all pro-Ally. Some, like the Morgan firm, were pro-British, and had been for years, while others, like Kuhn, Loeb and Company, manned chiefly by men of German derivation, were pro-German. But the financial interests of all the bankers soon came to be pro-Ally, for credit and loans to Germany were discouraged, while large loans were presently being made to the Allied powers.

On August 15, 1914, at the beginning of the war, Bryan declared against loans to any belligerent, on the ground that credit is the basis of all forms of contraband. President Wilson backed him up. For the time being, this position did not operate seriously against the Allies, for the balance of trade and investment was against the United States, and the Allied countries could pay for their purchases by cancelling the debts owed abroad by Americans. This situation took care of matters for a few months. But Allied war purchases became so great that, by the autumn of 1914, there was a credit crisis. The National City Bank addressed

Robert Lansing, then Counsellor of the State Department, on this matter on October 23, 1914. Short-term credits to European governments were advocated. Lansing talked the matter over with President Wilson at once, and the latter agreed that the government would not interfere with such an arrangement. This information was transmitted orally to Willard Straight of J. P. Morgan & Company at the Metropolitan Club in Washington on the same night.

Shortly afterwards, H. P. Davison of the Morgan firm went to England and signed a contract to become the British purchasing agent in America. A similar contract was soon made with France.

The short-term loans sufficed for some months, but by the summer of 1915 Allied buying had become so extensive that the bankers saw that they must float loans here for the Allied countries if the latter were to continue to buy American munitions on a large scale. So they made strong representations to Colonel House and to the Secretary of the Treasury, W. G. McAdoo.

On August 21, 1915, McAdoo wrote a long letter to President Wilson, pointing out that great prosperity had come to the country as a result of the sale of munitions to the Allies, but that this prosperity could not continue unless we financed it through open loans to the Allies—i.e. selling Allied bonds in our own financial markets.

On September 6, 1915, Secretary Lansing argued similarly in a letter to President Wilson, stressing the crisis that faced American business if the earlier ruling of Bryan and the President on American loans to belligerents was not rescinded. Colonel House supported this position. McAdoo and Lansing won their point. On September 8, 1915, Wilson assented to loans and the Morgan firm was once more given oral information. Very soon, the first public loan, the $500,000,000 Anglo-French loan, was floated.

The formal loans to the Allies—over $2,500,000,000 in all—financed their purchases for a little over a year, but their buying was so heavy that even the great investment banking houses could not take care of their needs. By January, 1917, the Allies had overdrawn their credit by nearly $500,000,000. Only Uncle Sam could save the great banking houses and the Allies. And Uncle Sam could help only if the United States were at war with Germany. We could not, as a government, lend money to a belligerent, unless we were at war with its enemy.

Just at this time the Germans renewed their unrestricted submarine warfare. The United States could now be led into the war, and the bankers would be repaid. They were repaid to the last cent. When the war was over, Mr. Thomas W. Lamont, of J. P. Morgan and Company, stated the facts relative to the attitude of his firm toward the World War and the belligerent powers:

At the request of certain of the foreign governments the firm of Messrs. J. P. Morgan and Company undertook to co-ordinate the requirements of the Allies, and then to bring about regularity and promptness in fulfilling these requirements. Those were the days when American citizens were being urged to remain neutral in action, in word, and even in thought. But our firm had never for one moment been neutral: we didn't know how to be. From the very start we did everything we could to contribute to the cause of the Allies. And this particular work had two effects: one in assisting the Allies in the production of goods and munitions in America necessary to the Allies' vigorous prosecution of the war; the other in helping to develop the great and profitable export trade that our country has had.

Most American industrialists naturally shared the attitude of the bankers. Since England controlled the seas, our sales were mainly to the Allied powers. We wished to see the Allies continue the war and win it. Upon their purchases depended most of our sales and prosperity, and upon their success and solvency depended the prospect of their being able to pay us in the end. The trade in munitions carried us from a depression in 1914 to boom years in 1915 and 1916.

By abandoning his neutral financial and industrial policy in favor of the Allies, President Wilson made it possible for the Entente Powers to enjoy an enormous advantage over the Central Powers in getting war supplies. The only way for the Central Powers to overcome it was to resume unlimited submarine warfare and try to sweep from the seas the ships that were carrying these supplies to the Allies.

It was our unneutral financing of the Allies that led to the resumption of German submarine warfare, and it was the resumption of this warfare which furnished the "incident" that enabled the war party in this country to put us into the conflict. It is, thus, perfectly clear that economic and financial pressure was the crucial factor which led us into war in 1917.

But no one need hold that President Wilson was moved primarily by any tender sentiments for the bankers. Both McAdoo and Lansing argued that it was essential to American prosperity to finance the Allies.

It was this general consideration of continued prosperity in 1915-16, and the relation of this to the prospects of the Democratic Party in the election of 1916, rather than any direct banker pressure on the White House, that bore in on

Wilson's consciousness in the late summer of 1915, when he let down the gates to financing the Allies.

Yet, it is downright silly to contend that the bankers had no influence on Wilson's policy. If he did not listen to the bankers himself, he did listen very attentively to those who did heed banker pressure, namely, McAdoo, Lansing and House.

The active campaign for American preparedness and intervention was engineered by leaders of the war cult in the United States, such men as Theodore Roosevelt, Leonard Wood, Henry Cabot Lodge, "Gus" Gardiner, and the like. They led in the preparedness movement, the Plattsburg camp episode, and other steps designed to stimulate the martial spirit in America. The newspapers warmly supported this movement because of the circulation appeal which preparedness material supplied.

While there were notable exceptions, the majority of our newspapers were pro-Ally and pro-interventionist. Many of them were honestly sympathetic with the Allies. Others were deeply influenced by Allied propaganda. Some were heavily subsidized by the Allies. Still others were bought outright by Allied interests. Moreover, the Allies supplied all American newspapers with a vast amount of war-news material always favorable to the Allied cause. The newspapers also had a natural affinity for the bankers and industrialists who were their chief advertising clients. Finally, the newspapers were not unaware of the enormous circulation gains and increased advertising revenue which would follow our entry into the World War.

In the matter of propaganda the Allies had a notable advantage. They controlled the seas, the cables, and other means of communication. The Germans had only one crude and temporary wireless contact with the United States. Further, Allied propaganda was far better organized and more lavishly supported. It was also much more adroit than the German. As a result, a majority of Americans were led to believe in the veracity of the great batch of atrocity lies relative to the German invasion of Belgium, submarine warfare, and the like. This was particularly true after Lord Bryce put the force of his name and prestige behind the authenticity of such tales. Lord Northcliffe, who was in charge of British propaganda, in moments of unusual candor, stated that the Americans proved more gullible in such matters than any other people except the Chinese and called us "a bunch of sheep."

The ministers of the gospel also joined heartily in the great crusade to put us into the World War. Lining up behind such a stalwart as Newell Dwight Hillis, they preached a veritable holy war. They represented the Allies as divinely-anointed promoters of international decency and justice and the Central Powers as the servants of evil and the agents of savagery.

The net result of all this was that we entered the World War in April, 1917. We did so, even though there was no clear legal or moral basis for our so doing. If there ever was an instance in which the facts were clearly in accord with a neutrality policy it was in the spring of 1917. We should have fought both Germany and Britain or else neither. But the country went into war, with most of the citizens of the United States feeling that our self-respect and national honor demanded it. No other course seemed open to us.

EDWIN BORCHARD (1884–1951), professor of law at Yale and author of several books and more than a score of articles on international law, stressed the legal aspects of neutrality in his study with William P. Lage, *Neutrality for the United States* (1937). Written while war clouds again cast a shadow over Europe and the American Congress debated neutrality legislation, the work is a plea for a policy of neutrality. Countering the internationalist argument that neutrality had failed to avert American involvement in World War I, Borchard argues that we were never neutral in that conflict, and that it was precisely our unneutrality that led to war. For him as for Barnes, the German submarine was not a cause but a response to the real cause of America's entry—its unneutrality.*

The Wages of Unneutrality

It is not a grateful task to record the diplomacy of the United States during the period 1914–17. Although President Wilson had enjoined on the nation the necessity for remaining neutral "in thought as well as in action," unfortunately he soon found himself entangled in an emotional drift toward intervention in the war. It is possible that he did not realize the extent to which he was committing himself. With little if any useful aid from Secretary Lansing, who seems to have fumbled nearly every legal issue, with an Ambassador in London who was less interested in his own country than in the success of what he supposed to be a crusade for civilization, and with a most adroit and effective propaganda operating to persuade the United States into seeing only one side of the issue, it required a strong, sophisticated, and detached mind, with a philosophical view of history, to resist the pressure and allurements to which President Wilson was subjected. Volumes have already been written, and more are likely to be written, analyzing the various factors which served to propel the United States into the European war. In this book no detailed examination of the diplomatic history of the time can be attempted; but it is possible to say that the conduct of the American Government during that period was a nega-

* From Edwin Borchard and William P. Lage, *Neutrality for the United States*, pp. 33–44, copyright 1937 by Yale University Press. Reprinted without footnotes by permission of the publisher.

tion of nearly all the requirements of neutrality both in thought and in action. The difficulty was not decreased by the profession that we were acting as neutrals, for neutrality and unneutrality became inextricably confused. There is no doubt that the administration desired to see the Allies win and declined to take any action even in defense of American neutral rights which would seriously interfere with that objective. Perhaps the objective is understandable—this is not the place to discuss that question—but to suggest that the objective was consistent with the maintenance of American neutrality is a travesty of the truth. We were unneutral and we paid the price.

Our unneutrality began as early as August, 1914. If neutrality was to be the national policy, the struggle to attain it, if such it was, did not last long. As we shall observe, the effort to obtain British adherence to the Declaration of London disclosed an obsequiousness on the part of Ambassador Page, Colonel House and Mr. Lansing which must have forfeited British respect for the American case and for the capacity of America's representatives to defend it. As Ray Stannard Baker says, "By October [1914], perhaps earlier, our case was lost."

Again, in the protest against the British "measures of blockade" which gradually exposed all American trade with the neutrals of Europe to British and Allied control, the United States as early as December, 1914, practically gave away the American case against Allied impositions with the pathetic admission that such trade could not be interfered with "unless such interference is manifestly an imperative necessity to protect their [Allied] national safety, and then

only to the extent that it is a necessity." The note appealed to "the deep sense of justice of the British nation" in requesting it to "refrain from all unnecessary interference with the freedom of trade" and to "conform more closely" to the rules of international law. But as long as the belligerents were to be the judges of "imperative necessity," this friendly admonition had the effect of acquiescing in their illegal measures. The British seem so to have construed it. Baker remarks: ". . . One cannot avoid the impression, after a careful study of this document, that the Administration's defense of American policy was in reality a defense of the British blockade, and furnished the British government with a whole arsenal of arguments against our own criticism of that blockade."

Although on August 18, 1914, President Wilson had solemnly urged "every man who really loves America" to "act and speak in the true spirit of neutrality, which is the spirit of impartiality . . . and friendliness to all concerned," and had warned against "partisanship" and "taking sides," on August 30, 1914, only twelve days later, he is recorded as telling Colonel House "that if Germany won, it would change the course of our civilization and make the United States a military nation."

The submarine campaign initiated by Germany in February, 1915, seems to have deeply offended President Wilson and to have fixed his attachment to the Allied cause. This influenced both the tone and contents of his notes to Germany and he began to talk about "strict accountability." Even before the *Lusitania* sinking in May, 1915, Attorney General Gregory attended a Cabinet meeting which he described as follows:

While these conditions existed [i.e., the sinking of ships before the *Lusitania*] a cabinet meeting was held, at which several of Mr. Wilson's advisers expressed great indignation at what they considered violation [by Britain] of our international rights, and urged a more vigorous policy on our part.

After patiently listening, Mr. Wilson said, in that quiet way of his, that the ordinary rules of conduct had no application to the situation; that the Allies were standing with their backs to the wall, fighting wild beasts; that he would permit nothing to be done by our country to hinder or embarrass them in the prosecution of the war unless admitted rights were grossly violated, and that this policy must be understood as settled.

Like all true-hearted Americans, he hoped that the United States would not be drawn into the war; but he was of Scotch and English blood, and by inheritance, tradition and rearing at all times the friend of the Allies.

On September 22, 1915, Colonel House records Wilson's views as follows: "Much to my surprise, he [Wilson] said he had never been sure that we ought not to take part in the conflict, and, if it seemed evident that Germany and her militaristic ideas were to win, the obligation upon us was greater than ever."

Mr. Tumulty, the President's Secretary, reports the President as believing that the public demand that he keep England within legal bounds was actuated by a "sinister political purpose." The President is reported to have approved Sir Edward Grey's statement that "of course many of the restrictions that we have laid down and which seriously interfere with your trade are unreasonable, but America must remember that we are fighting her fight as well as our own to save the civilization of the world." The President thereupon adopted this idea as his own, stating, according to Mr. Tumulty: "England is fighting our fight and you may well understand that I shall not, in the present state of affairs, place obstacles in her way." He declined to take any action to embarrass England when she "is fighting for her life and the life of the world."

Secretary Lansing admits in his *Memoirs* that as early as July, 1915, he had concluded that "the German Government is utterly hostile to all nations with democratic institutions" and that "Germany must not be permitted to win this war or to break even, though to prevent it this country is forced to take an active part. This ultimate necessity must be constantly in our minds in all our controversies with the belligerents. American public opinion must be prepared for the time, which may come, when we will have to cast aside our neutrality and become one of the champions of democracy."

We shall have occasion to see that the legal positions of the United States in its controversies with the belligerents were highly colored by this view, to which Mr. Lansing gave repeated expression. Describing his notes to England, Mr. Lansing says:

The notes that were sent were long and exhaustive treatises which opened up new subjects of discussion rather than closing those in controversy. Short and emphatic notes were dangerous. Everything was submerged in verbosity. It was done with deliberate purpose. It insured continuance of the controversies and left the questions unsettled, which was necessary in order to leave this country free to act and even to act illegally when it entered the war.

On October 6, 1915, Colonel House wrote to Mr. Page: "We have given the Allies our sympathy and we have given them, too, the more substantial help that we could not offer Germany even were we so disposed—and that is an unrestricted amount of munitions of war and money. In addition to that, we have forced Germany to discontinue her submarine warfare . . ." In 1915, Mr. Lansing wrote to Colonel House: "In no event should we take a course that would seriously endanger our friendly relations with Great Britain, France, or Russia, for, as you say, our friendship with Germany is a thing of the past."

On January 11, 1916, Colonel House records a conference he held with British leaders in which they had asked "what the United States wished Great Britain to do." To this the neutral Colonel replied: "The United States would like Great Britain to do those things which would enable the United States to help Great Britain win the war." Page admired this "cleverness."

And Mr. Lansing discloses at least one reason for his insincere defense of American neutrality, by stating: "in dealing with the British Government there was always in my mind the conviction that we would ultimately become an ally of Great Britain." His point of view being that of a prospective ally, his conduct was in reasonable accord.

No wonder that Sir Cecil Spring-Rice's biographer could say of him: "As to his value in negotiation, it cannot be overlooked that during the period while America was neutral, all the issues in dispute between England and America were decided as England wished." And Lord Reading adds: "I believe it to be the case that the Allied governments were never forced to recede from their position in any important question owing to American opposition."

The American surrender was, unfortunately, not merely a betrayal of neutrality, of which Lansing declared we were to be the "champions"; it was a surrender of the independence of the United States and of American self-respect. Furthermore, it must have forfeited the respect of Great Britain and her Allies. The surrender was not made through malevolence but through short-sighted emotionalism, a confusion of ideas as to where America's interest lay. It set the mood for that partiality and that incapacity to take and stand upon correct legal positions which ultimately made of the United States an instrument of the foreign policy of certain European belligerents.

We need only refer to the agreement between Colonel House and Sir Edward Grey on February 22, 1916 (of all days!), for the contingent intervention of the United States on behalf of the Allies if the Central Powers failed to accept terms of peace suitable to the Allies. Such an agreement is unique in the history of "neutrality."

Nor need more than passing reference be made to the "Sunrise Breakfast Conference" in April, 1916, in which President Wilson sought to find out from Speaker Clark, Floor Leader Kitchin, and Chairman Flood of the Foreign Affairs Committee of the House whether Congress could be persuaded to approve war against Germany.

It is now established that the British Ambassador was often notified in advance that important notes of protest against British violations of American rights were merely formal and not to be taken too seriously. In connection with the American note of October 21, 1915, Ambassador Spring-Rice was requested to send Sir Edward Grey a cable preparing him for a protest. Spring-Rice assured his government that the note was due to the fact that "the United States must defend their rights and they must make a good showing before Congress meets, but that the correspondence should not take a hostile character but should be in the nature of a juridical discussion."

An entirely different attitude distinguishes the correspondence of the United States with Great Britain from that with Germany. Had there been no fundamental prejudice in favor of one group of belligerents, the legal questions might have been approached with greater felicity and understanding.

On the armed merchantmen question, the unsustainable position was taken that, notwithstanding the ability of a single shot to sink a submarine and notwithstanding the British Admiralty orders to ram or fire on submarines at sight, nevertheless the submarine had no right to fire on and sink an armed belligerent merchantman which had American citizens on board. Thus, the neutral United States undertook to defend British merchantmen from attack by their enemy, a practice new in history. The real legal issues involved in the *Lusitania* case—her naval status, her cargo, her course in the war zone, the risks the passengers assumed—were not carefully examined, but ultimata were sent to Germany which were not and have not since been justified. The administration declined to inform American citizens, notwithstanding Secretary Bryan's importunities, that they took passage on belligerent vessels at their own risk. It fought the Gore-McLemore Resolutions of 1916 which merely sought to declare this elementary rule of law.

No more than casual reference needs to be made to one of the more egregious lurches into unneutrality, whereby the United States and its people were led into financing the munitions supply of one set of the belligerents, the Allies. In August, 1914, the administration had announced that the flotation of loans for the belligerents was "inconsistent with the spirit of neutrality." In October, 1914, as the munitions traffic developed, a plausible argument was advanced by Mr. Lansing that bank credits for the purchase of supplies were not public loans and hence should not be banned. The President agreed, but was not willing to let the public know that he had approved this qualification of his original position. By August, 1915, this trade had developed to such proportions that the credits needed to be funded and, it was argued, the Allied governments had to have new money to buy their enormous supplies. The 1914 prohibition and its reasons stood in the way. The Secretary of the Treasury made an eloquent plea to the President for authority to permit the Federal Reserve banks to discount bills and acceptances, a flagrantly unneutral act of the United States Government, and to permit the Allied governments to float loans in the United States. Again the President yielded, but again not publicly. He thus committed himself to a policy which could have but one end, for as the need for Allied credit continued—the argument was that American prosperity could not be permitted to decline—and private lenders became reluctant, only public lending could meet the need, and that meant war. Like the impressment issue to the "War Hawks" of 1812, the German submarine note of January 31, 1917, must have been a godsend to the interventionists. The way to the public Treasury was now open. The subsequent record is current history.

The strange thing is that President Wilson apparently failed to perceive that he was inveigled from one misstep to the next and that the end of the trail was intervention. Perhaps his mental attitude in August, 1915, was already such that he conceived it legitimate to reverse Secretary Bryan's and his own sensible position of August, 1914. Those members of the Federal Reserve Board who in August, 1915, were reluctant to permit the Federal Reserve banks' participation in this violation of neutrality were denounced by Secretary McAdoo as "pro-German," then as later a form of psychological terrorism to discourage the well-balanced, the thoughtful, the really neutral devotees of America, its traditions and its independence. The remarkable fact is that under the impact of the mighty forces making for American involvement, including the consistently unneutral attitude of mind and action of the leaders of the administration, American intervention was nevertheless delayed for more than two years. That fact alone attests the fundamental detachment of the American people and their aversion to participation in European wars.

No wonder that the belated effort of President Wilson in December, 1916, to end the war fell in England on unresponsive ears. The British Government had no reason to believe that the United States would exert pressure on England or that it would even act impartially. The mediatory or constructive influence of the United States had been frittered away; only its physical power as a belligerent was now sought. That ultimate seduction was not difficult.

Great Britain, well aware of the situation in Washington, timed its replies so as to conceal the downright refusal of practically every American protest; they were almost invariably delivered when the administration was engrossed in the clouds of controversy incidental to American protests against the German submarine. Thus, the American note of October 21, 1915, was answered on April 19, 1916, when the *Sussex* controversy was at its height. This was excellent strategy, like the release of the Bryce reports on German atrocities in Belgium at the time of the *Lusitania* controversy. In like manner, Great Britain made cotton absolute contraband on August 20, 1915, the day following the sinking of the British steamer *Arabic*.

It is not necessary to extend the demonstration of American unneutrality by a discussion of the feeble protest at the seizure of American mails and the diversion of all northern transatlantic shipping into British ports for examination. Nor is it necessary to discuss the forcible removal of passengers from American ships on the high seas if they were thought to be German reservists.

President Wilson thought the "national honor" required him to fight for the right of American citizens to take passage unmolested on British merchant ships. As John Bassett Moore stated to the Senate Foreign Relations Committee in 1936: "We became involved in war directly as the result of our undertaking to guarantee the safety of belligerent merchantmen and our taking the position that armed belligerent merchantmen were to be considered as peaceful vessels." It is not necessary to emphasize the fact that scarcely a ton of cargo left an American port from 1915 to 1917 without the control of a British agent. And we need merely call attention to the submission of the United States to the impositions of the British black list which prevented an American citizen from trading with Germans or even Chileans in Chile if their names had been placed on the British black lists—this at a time when Canada refused to submit to such a black list and freely sent shipments to those very firms!

This brief record justifies a few comments. Those who wish to confer on the Executive a wide discretion to embargo commodities during the course of a foreign war may well observe how Executive discretion was employed in 1914–17. Another striking fact to observe is that all the policies for which Mr. Bryan stood—the embargo on arms and munitions, a prohibition on loans, a prohibition to travel on belligerent ships except at the traveler's risk—policies which the rest of the administration firmly opposed, have now received the practically unanimous support of Congress and of the present [Franklin Roosevelt] administration. Mr. Bryan looms larger as a statesman and a prophet. It must also be evident that mere lip service to the yearning to keep out of war, which was as evident during the period 1914–17 as it is now, is no guaranty against partisan policies that have as a natural effect precipitating American entanglement. It may fairly be said that our foreign policy in 1914–17 was, in major matters, consistently unneutral and in some respects, as on the armed merchantmen question, legally unsustainable.

No one can blame the British Government for adroitly safeguarding its own interests and by a most astute propaganda playing on American naïveté, using the United States as an instrument of its national policy. Its intelligence and skill are to be envied. Great Britain's activities are not to be resented because the leaders and people of the United States permitted themselves to be persuaded by British statesmen to enter suicidal paths in the interests of the Higher Morality or "Civilization" or the "Life of the World." But the record of American statesmanship speaks for itself, as do the results.

Unlike Barnes and Borchard, H. C. PETERSON (1902–1952) did not set out to prove that the United States was unneutral: accepting this as fact, he sought to show *why* it was. His book, which grew out of a Ph.D. dissertation on American entry into the war, attributes the unneutrality of the United States and its resulting involvement to the power and influence of British propaganda. A staunch opponent of the war, Peterson was at work on a study of American opponents of World War I at the time of his death. His manuscript has since been completed, substantially revised, and published by Professor Gilbert C. Fite, Peterson's friend and colleague at the University of Oklahoma.*

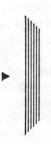

Propaganda as the Cause of War

The British campaign to induce the United States to come to their assistance affected every phase of American life; it was propaganda in its broadest meaning. News, money, and political pressure each played its part and the battle itself was fought not only in London, New York, and Washington, D. C., but also in American classrooms and pulpits, factories, and offices. It was a campaign to create a pro-British attitude of mind among Americans, to get American sympathies and interests so deeply involved in the European war that it would be impossible for this country to remain neutral.

The first problem confronting the directors of any such campaign was that of winning the sympathy of the general public. When Lord Northcliffe visited this country he remarked of Americans: "They dress alike, they talk alike, they think alike. What sheep!" Although he was not entirely correct, he was right in that the American public, like any public, demands uniformity of thought and conformity of action. In so far as Americans were sheep they had to be reached through their emotions. Although every public thinks with its hopes, its fears, and its affections, the pre-war American public was especially sentimental, excessively turbulent in comparison with European, and finally, was subject

* From *Propaganda for War: The Campaign Against American Neutrality, 1914–1917*, by H. C. Peterson. Copyright 1939 by the University of Oklahoma Press. Pp. 4–9, 12–17, 25–28, 32, 326. Footnotes accompanying this selection in the original have been omitted by permission of the publisher.

to waves of emotion, apathy, interest, and boredom. The work of the British propagandist was to harness these feelings and put them to work for the Allies.

The British propaganda campaign naturally had to be based upon ideas Americans already had concerning the belligerent nations. In the first place it was soon found that people in the United States had but slight interest in countries other than those in Western Europe. Any "educational" efforts had to turn upon those lands west of the Vistula and north of the Danube. Among these, Germany was held in high esteem, but, fortunately for the Allies, this esteem had been diminished by certain actions of the German government after 1870. By the turn of the century, in some quarters, this had developed into positive dislike. The visit of Prince Henry, the Kaiser's brother, in 1902, occasioned somewhat of an outburst against Germany, but "it is interesting to note that the papers most vigorously assailing the Prince were often those of undisguised British sympathies." France was neither liked nor disliked. Her underdog position and the fact that she had assisted this country during the Revolutionary War created some sympathy but, to the average churchgoer, the French seemed a trifle wicked. Belgium was practically unknown, which was an advantage. England, up to 1914, had been the most popular enemy of Americans. People in the United States enjoyed disliking her, but it was the dislike of first cousins. The distinct advantage, in so far as Anglo-Amreican relations were involved, was that Americans thought they and the English were members of the same cultural scheme. The language factor here played a tremendously im-

portant part. Among many elements in the country there existed a tendency to be very friendly toward England, and even among those who disliked the British there was to be found a feeling of respect for "our English cousins."

The problem of gaining the sympathy and support of the American public turned upon the attitude of American newspapers. Here the British were greatly assisted by pre-war relations between the American press and the press of Great Britain. "For years the American public had received its day-by-day picture of Europe through a distinctly British perspective. Few American newspapers at that time maintained European staffs of their own; while those which did found few trained American foreign correspondents to man them. There were one or two capable American newspapermen in Berlin, but there were probably none at all in St. Petersburg, while even the Paris correspondents concentrated mainly upon social and artistic news rather than political reporting. Both our newspapers and press associations tended to cover European politics from London. Their London bureaus had general supervision over the correspondents on the Continent; the news was largely assembled in the London bureaus and forwarded by them. It was often heavily filled out with information or 'background' material derived from the British newspapers and magazines simply because they had so much better sources than the American staffs. . . . The New York *Times,* which perhaps gave more serious attention to European events than any other American newspaper, had an Englishman, Mr. Ernest Marshall, as the head of its London bureau, and his subordinates were largely Britishers. Its

Berlin correspondent, Mr. Frederick William Wile, was an American, but the *Times* shared him with Northcliffe's *Daily Mail,* a leader in the anti-German propaganda in England. The New York *World*'s London correspondent was an Irishman who had never worked in the United States; his staff, like Mr. Marshall's, was largely composed of British newspapermen. So was that of the *Sun.* Those correspondents who were American citizens, moreover, had often lived so long abroad as to absorb the British viewpoint. The dean of the American correspondents in London, Mr. Edward Price Bell of the Chicago *Daily News,* had arrived fresh from college, to remain there for the rest of his active life, and it was naturally impossible for the others not to reflect the atmosphere by which they were daily surrounded." The result was "that the American view of Europe was normally and unavoidably colored very deeply by the British attitude."

The problem of the press within the United States was much more complicated and much more important. American newspapers in the first two decades of the century were the dominant factor in controlling opinion. They comprised the sole reading material for ninety per cent of the American people. German propagandists informed their home office that "everything must be communicated to the American public in the form of 'news' as they have been accustomed to this, and only understand this kind of propaganda." Propagandists probably also realized that the American newspapers deal only incidentally with news —that their principal commodity is sensation. In case of a foreign war, the support of the press would tend to go to the side which provided the best sensations. This, of course, meant that newspapers were very undependable. Like the public, the American press is a volatile force. . . .

Finally, it should be borne in mind that the press bureaus and the great Eastern dailies exert a disproportionate influence on the American press as a whole. During the war years there were about twenty-five hundred daily papers in the United States. About a thousand of these were affiliated with the Associated Press and most of the rest were connected with the United Press or one of the other press organizations—all of which were dominated by prominent New York editors. The foreign news which came through these bureaus was primarily composed for the New York newspapers, so, in the last analysis, the control of the New York press practically meant the control of the entire American press.

The immediate problem for the British propagandists at the outset of the war was to obtain the support of the leaders of American life. In this regard they were very fortunate. The American aristocracy was distinctly Anglophile. To assume a pro-British attitude was the "thing to do" among cultured Americans. "Politicians might placate an Irish constituency or stir our bumptious nationalism with a little tail-twisting now and then; but those more cultivated elements which dominated our intellectual, political and financial life still found in London their unacknowledged capital." This was accentuated by the fact that the economic aristocracy did most of its foreign business through London. Nearly all foreign banking was handled through the English capital. One of the Morgan partners stated: "Like most of our contemporaries and friends and neighbors, we wanted the Allies to win the war from the outset.

We were pro-Ally by inheritance, by instinct, by opinion."

The intellectual leaders of the United States were also sympathetic toward England, largely as a result of the similarity of language and the fact that England was the one foreign country with which most of them were acquainted. College professors, ministers, and above all, public school teachers, saw in England all that they thought was missing from America; consequently they lavished upon her a great deal of affection.

The problem of winning the support of the political leaders of the United States appeared to be even less difficult than that of gaining the adherence of the economic, social, and intellectual leaders. Primarily politicians are reflectors of opinion, and the opinions they reflect are usually those given in the press. . . .

The agencies and organizations by means of which the British influenced the thinking of the American people were many and varied. Some, such as censorship and intelligence groups, were formally organized, but many of the most effective agencies were independent and connected with no responsible propaganda department. It would be impossible to list all the groups which spread British ideas about the war because, in the last analysis, all people who had been propagandized were doing this work. However, it is possible to deal with the major sections, or units, which were fighting the war of words.

The first propaganda organization to be set in motion was that of censorship. On August 5, 1914, the British cut the cables between Germany and the United States. No other means of rapid communication existed between these two

nations, and as a result, the most effective instrument of propaganda, the news, was suppressed at the most crucial time in the history of the war—the time when first impressions were being made, when opinions were being established. Even after the inauguration of trans-Atlantic wireless, late in 1914, with its limited facilities for the transmission of news, German dispatches were slower than the British so that even the later, less important British interpretations of events became the accepted versions in America.

In November, 1917, an official of the State Department wrote to President Wilson advocating a censorship of the American press. His principal argument was that "the *first publication* is that which is *formative of public opinion* and which affects public emotion." By controlling these first impressions all the opponent could do was to "retrieve part of the unfortunate effect" created by the original publication, and, in words of one British propaganda agent, "no contradiction, no retraction, can quite overcome the harm of the first printing."

The cutting of the cables between the United States and Germany was the first act of censorship and the first act of propaganda. These Siamese twins of public opinion were from that time to dictate what the American people were to think. The second move in the same endeavor was the censorship of the press of England. This was done under the Defense of the Realm Act, the famous DORA, which gave control over "all statements intended or likely to prejudice His Majesty's relations with foreign powers." The year before the war there had been formed a Joint Consultative Committee of Admiralty, War Office, and Press for the purpose of planning censorship. This Press Censorship Committee was replaced in August, 1916, by the Press Bureau with its duty to "supervise, largely on a voluntary basis, issue of news to and by the press." Sir John Simon, the Home Secretary, was responsible to the Cabinet, while in direct charge was F. E. Smith, the later Lord Birkenhead. He was replaced on September 3, 1914, by Stanley Buckmaster. It must be remembered, of course, that in addition to this committee, nearly every department of the British government maintained its own separate intelligence and censorship bureau.

As a matter of fact, the Press Bureau "was only a shield and recording angel for the naval and military censors who acted under direct instructions from the Admiralty and War Office." As one Englishman remarked, it was "the imaginative department, the body which dresses up the facts for presentment to the public, a most important function and one leaving scope for individual imagination." This censorship bureau in Great Britain must be considered a determining factor in controlling American opinion, because the news which it passed was the version which the American press released.

With their German source of information cut off, American newspapers had to secure their war news where it was available—and that was from England. The only way they could get even partially complete European news was to buy the advance sheets of London newspapers. Otherwise they were limited to official communiqués from the British or French governments. News obtained from other European countries also had to be filtered through the British censorship, so it can be seen that it was truly the British news that became American news. The American correspondents in Europe did attempt to send unbiased

news to their papers. They struggled against the restrictions imposed upon them by the British, but to no avail —they were helpless victims of circumstance. "Schreiner of the Associated Press estimated that at this time [1915] nearly three-quarters of the dispatches written by American correspondents in Central Europe were perishing under the shears of the British censors."

The censorship of mail, similar to censorship of press and cable, served to control information passing between Europe and America. It also served as a source of information for the propagandists. The British mail censorship started on August 29, 1914, with fourteen persons on the original staff. By Easter of 1916 it had a force of approximately two thousand. Early in 1917 there were thirty-seven hundred persons in London alone censoring mail, and fifteen hundred in Liverpool. Colonel G. S. H. Pearson was Chief Postal Censor from 1914 to 1918. The main office of this group was in Salisbury House in London but most of its work was done at the Liverpool branch. There were also censors at Gibraltar, Alexandria, and Folkestone. In each case the censorship bureau consisted of a military and naval room, a cable department, and an issuing department. This last had charge of information to be turned over to the press.

Utilizing this censorship with great intelligence, the British were able to keep tab on all their enemies and the friends of their enemies. The censor summarized all information of interest which his organization intercepted and sent his reports to the departments which would be interested in the particular intelligence. It can readily be seen that such a source of information would be invaluable for every phase of propaganda work. It is also apparent that the elimination of information would cripple enemy propaganda. Occasionally the *Confidential Supplement* of the *Daily Review of the Foreign Press* would include information taken from "intercepted letters."

One British measure of immense importance to the propagandists, indirectly connected with censorship, was the interception of wireless messages to and from Germany. Eventually the staff taking care of this work grew to about fifty "and as many as 2,000 intercepted messages were often received and dealt with in 24 hours." "In 1916 the Germans contracted a habit of changing the key of the principal Naval Signal Book every night at 12 o'clock, but the deciphering staff of Room 40 had by that time become so expert that the changes caused the night watch no serious embarrassment." The work was done by the Naval Intelligence Department under Admiral Sir William Reginald Hall; the man in direct charge was Sir Alfred Ewing. The intelligence intercepted in this way was invaluable to propagandists as well as to statesmen and enabled the British government to anticipate many of the moves of her enemies.

The foregoing censorship controls could be called negative propaganda; they made it possible for the positive propaganda to achieve a more complete victory. In fact, it is difficult to see how the propagandists could have operated without the censor.

In September, 1914, Charles Masterman was authorized by the British Foreign Office to form a War Propaganda Bureau. Installed in Wellington House, the office of an insurance firm, it began to issue the propaganda which was soon to flood the United States. Developing by leaps and bounds, it became the principal outlet for books, pamphlets, and other instruments of British propaganda. Each branch of the work was controlled by a separate department under the direction of some individual of considerable prominence. Mr. Eric Maclagan was in charge of propaganda for France; Mr. William Archer directed the department for the Scandinavian countries; while Sir Gilbert Parker supervised the one which took care of propaganda for the United States—the American Ministry of Information. Parker had as his assistants Professor Macneile Dixon of Glasgow University, Mr. A. J. Toynbee of Balliol College, and others. Starting out with nine men, by 1917 he had fifty-four.

The mailing list of Wellington House (as a whole), being carefully compiled was expanded till it contained 260,000 names of influential persons throughout the Union." Sir Gilbert Parker's list was made after consulting the American *Who's Who*. From this compilation he made separate groupings of prominent Americans, according to their profession, supposed intelligence, or standing in the community.

Nicholson has stated that "Wellington house was . . . concerned with the production, translation and distribution of books, pamphlets, government publications, speeches and so forth dealing with the war, its origin, its history and all the varied and difficult questions which arose during its development; the production and distribution of special pictorial papers; assisting in the placing of articles and interviews designed to influence opinion in the world's newspapers and magazines, especially in America; the wide distribution of pictorial matter, cartoons, pictures and drawings, photographs for insertion in newspapers and periodicals and for exhibition; the production and distribution of cinematograph films; personal correspondence with influential people abroad, especially in America; arrangements for the interchange of visits, of personal tours to neutral and allied countries and of visits of distinguished neutrals and of representatives of the Allies to this country; the production and distribution of maps, diagrams, posters, lantern slides and lectures, pictures, postcards, and all other possible means of miscellaneous propaganda."

Sir Gilbert Parker has remarked that "besides our private correspondence with individuals we had our literature sent to a great number of public libraries, Y.M.C.A. societies, universities, colleges, clubs, and newspapers.". . .

Just as they used natives in Africa and Asia, the British did all in their power to enlist Americans as propagandists to overcome the resistance of Americans. One distinguished English expert in this field wrote: "Better than any pumped-in propaganda abroad was [the] . . . method of making the leaders of the Imperial, neutral or Allied press themselves the propagandists when they returned home." In doing this the British did not attempt bribery. Instead, the "method chosen was that of direct personal approach." Most educated Englishmen are socially delightful and in this phase of propaganda they were able to put their charm to work to good advantage. There is a compulsion in friendship which makes disagreement very distasteful and before long the British had eliminataed "disagreement" from their American friends.

Sir Gilbert Parker has stated that he "advised and stimulated many people to write articles" and "asked . . . friends and correspondents to arrange for speeches, debates and lectures by American citizens." Especially did he utilize

the "friendly services and assistance of confidential friends." Here was the real genius of British propaganda organization. In other circles this procedure would be called a "confidence game." Eventually, as a result of the propaganda and the campaign to get the friendship of American leaders, almost all articulate Americans were taken into the Allies' camp, to become Crusaders for England.

The first of the "native" propagandists were newspapermen. Their enlistment was, in origin, quite accidental. In order to make the stifling of news more acceptable to the dissatisfied correspondents, an "official eye-witness" at the front had been appointed by the British. His efforts pleased no one. In March and April, 1915, a step forward was made when parties of British correspondents were taken on a tour of the battlefields. In doing this it was discovered that the news writers could be pacified and at the same time be made to serve as propagandists. By stationing the reporters at the various army headquarters, and by making them personal friends, they became apologists for the British cause. In June, 1915, when the British General Headquarters received one American (Frederick Palmer) and six British correspondents, this system of propaganda was formally started.

After this, the British propagandists constantly had the American newspapermen in mind. Nicholson has stated that Wellington House was vitally interested in "helping to provide information and facilities to London correspondents of neutral, especially American, papers." In 1916 Wellington House endorsed the recommendations of one of its agents that "special correspondents from this country [the United States] . . . should be sent to the front and be allowed to see actual fighting." Explaining, he stated: "The French have, on the surface, done no propaganda work of any kind" but have been very cordial to American correspondents in France "and these correspondents have come back here and written the most enthusiastic articles for France. The last and most convincing . . . is to be found in the visit of Frank Simonds." The British went even further; they entertained all people of importance who visited France. "Editors, novelists, political experts, essayists, statesmen, university presidents, and men of importance in all walks of life, especially Americans, were given tours of the front. A visitor's chateau was provided for them and there the cuisine was excellent, while food rationing in England tightened under the growing submarine menace. They were chaperoned by most attentive and diplomatic reserve officers who had notes in hand from the Foreign Office about the standing and character of each visitor which made ingratiating hospitality the easier on the part of hosts. The guests were shown what was good for them to see. . . ."

Back in England, "American journalists, publicists, authors, statesmen, greeters, and munition-makers" were courted assiduously. "Clubs were open to them, teas and dinners were given for them." "The American wives of Englishmen, who had already given their proof that blood is thicker than water, led by Lady Astor, formed a battalion of solicitude lest Americans in London become homesick."

John St. Loe Strachey had a meeting of American correspondents each week at his home in London. There reporters were given the opportunity to meet some important personage, such as a cabinet member or a military leader. Men formerly aloof and inaccessible to reporters became very cordial. The personal contacts established at these meetings made censorship less distasteful to the correspondents, and also made it more difficult for those attending to give any but a British interpretation of news —even if it had been possible to get such a version past the censor. The same type of meeting was held by the foreign editor of the London *Times*.

In order to exert the same influence over American press bureaus, the British Naval Censor kept "in closest touch" with the British agents of the Associated Press (Mr. Collins) and the United Press (Mr. Keen). The European press bureaus had, of course, already been turned into propaganda agencies. The British had Reuters while the French used Havas. Even the German colonies had to copy their news from the dispatches of these two organizations. Reuters sent out more than a million words a month, making up every week approximately four hundred articles.

In conducting such a propaganda system of native workers, it was necessary to go beyond those important individuals whom they could reach in Europe. In order to influence those small newspapers in the United States which had no press service and no correspondents abroad, Sir Gilbert Parker, "supplied three hundred and sixty newspapers in the smaller cities of the United States with an English newspaper which [gave] a weekly review and comment of the affairs of the war."

Few opportunities to influence writers were left unexploited and although newspaper people objected strongly to the control which was placed upon them, their resistance was unavailing. News was essential to the success of their papers and in order to secure news they had to conform—which they did. The almost complete capture of American newswriters resulted in a press consistently friendly to the Allies. The American division of the British propaganda ministry made a weekly analysis of this success for the information of the Cabinet. A terse statement such as, "The week supplies satisfactory evidence of the permeation of the American press by British influence" means a great deal more in this connection than would seem at first glance. It means that even British propagandists were satisfied with their control.

But newspaper people were not the only Americans who were enlisted to fight Britain's battles. Appeal was systematically made to all classes. One discussion of this problem divided Americans first as to "particular faiths"; second, "particular nationalities"; third, "labor"; fourth, "intellectuals"; and fifth, the "average man." In all these cases it should be remembered that the motive was to secure the active support of the leaders of that particular class. . . .

The great success of British propaganda in the United States should not be attributed to a professional group of propagandists but to native Americans —volunteer propagandists. These were individually enlisted in some cases, but in the main were regimented into "soldiers of the king" by a process of eliminating, or at least curtailing, enemy interpretations of the war and by dominating the news with exaggerated and warped pro-Ally accounts of what was happening or had happened. Once these natives had acquired the "correct" frame of mind, they were enlisted for the "duration of the war." The formal propaganda groups acted merely as connecting and reinforcing elements of the British propaganda organizations. The real propagandists were Americans—our preachers, teachers, politicians, and journalists. . . .

The reasons back of the American decision of April, 1917, were not unlike those which had governed the European nations in the crisis of August, 1914. There was the same overcharged atmosphere of hate and distrust; there was the same helplessness resulting from an entanglement of interests; and there was the same stubbornness and political ineptitude on the part of the statesmen. Even the immediate cause for American entrance into the war was brought about by a political impasse similar to that of 1914. Like Grey, Poincaré, and the Kaiser, the American and German officials had taken an extreme position from which they could not retreat without a loss of prestige to themselves and their nations. Wilson, like his European contemporaries, chose war rather than accept a diplomatic defeat, and, again like them, justified himself by claiming that the United States was entering the war to uphold peace, liberty, democracy, and the rights of small nations.

The most important of the reasons for the American action in 1917, however, was none of these things—it was instead the attitude of mind in this country— the product of British propaganda. People under the influence of the propaganda came to look upon the struggle of 1914–18 as a simple conflict between the forces of good and evil; they felt that all that was wrong was that certain malevolent individuals had gained control of an autocratic government and were attempting to dictate to the rest of the world. In the minds of American leaders there was developed a blind hatred of everything German. After this hatred had distorted American neutrality, it created a willingness to sacrifice American youth in an attempt to punish the hated nation.

Author of several standard monographs on American foreign affairs, CHARLES CALLAN TANSILL (1890–1964) stands in the forefront of Revisionist writers on both World Wars. A professor of history at Georgetown and Fordham, he devoted ten years to the research and writing of *America Goes to War* (1938), finally giving up his teaching position in order to complete it. The selection from that work reprinted below emphasizes the economic causes of American involvement. Tansill, of course, wrote with the assumption common to all Revisionists, that America's entry was a mistake. Would it be possible to accept Tansill's evidence but, operating on a contrary assumption, come to a different conclusion? In other words, is the quarrel between the Revisionists and others over evidence, assumptions, or both?*

▶ *War Profits and Unneutrality*

Within a few weeks after the outbreak of the World War it became apparent to competent military observers that victory for either side would largely depend upon the possession of adequate supplies of munitions of war. The nation that labored under the greatest handicap in this regard was Great Britain, whose assistance to France in the early months of the war was sharply limited because of a glaring deficiency in effective artillery and in high explosive shells. Although the production of British factories could be rapidly increased there would remain an alarming shortage of supplies necessary for the conduct of successful warfare. The only means of meeting this situation was through the importation of munitions of war from neutral nations. European neutrals, however, soon placed embargoes upon the shipment of war materials, so the British Government was forced to look to America as the only important neutral that could supply her needs.

In America the rise of "big business" had produced a vast industrial organization that could fill war orders in an amazingly short time, and the very fact that this organization was severely suffering from a widespread business depression meant that these orders would receive special attention. It was not long before immense exports of American

* From *America Goes to War* by Charles Callan Tansill, pp. 32, 53–66, 69–78, 134, by permission of Little, Brown and Co. Footnotes omitted by permission of publisher. Copyright 1938 by Charles Callan Tansill.

munitions were crowding British ports. In 1916 the value of American war supplies to the Allied Governments amounted to more than a billion dollars, and the intimate economic ties thus created served to supplement the sentimental bonds that had long attached America to the side of the Entente Powers. . . .

One of the most significant aspects of the rapid growth in the export of American munitions of war to the Allied Powers is the close relationship between this trade and the economic situation in the United States during the years from 1913 to 1915. The first months of the Wilson Administration ushered in a widespread business depression which the far-reaching domestic program of the new Chief Executive seemed to intensify rather than dispel. The outbreak of the World War in August, 1914, made matters considerably worse, and the outlook for economic recovery was distinctly gloomy. Many factories were working at merely sixty per cent. capacity. Estimates of the unemployed reached close to a million, with a hundred thousand of these idle men near the starvation level.

An important side-light on business conditions is given in the following letter from Andrew Carnegie to President Wilson, November 23, 1914:—

The present Financial and Industrial situations are very distressing. I have never known such conditions, such pressing calls upon debtors to pay, and especially to reduce mortgages. Saturday morning last my Secretary reported forty-five appeals to me to meet such calls in one delivery—to-day he tells me that we shall have a hundred or more *at least*. This may change slowly, the Allies purchases from us from Horses down, are certain to be great.

When the Allied Governments began to place in the United States large orders for war materials an improvement in business conditions was soon manifest. But "hard times" persisted well into 1915 with recovery always a little doubtful. In January, 1915, the *Commercial and Financial Chronicle* believed that the "worst is undoubtedly behind us and there is occasion for rejoicing that it is." In March, 1915, some cautious editors still remained a little skeptical about returning prosperity, and *Commerce and Finance* sagely remarked that "the exuberance at first excited by the unprecedented balance in our favor is giving place to an appreciation of the truth that we cannot hope to be permanently prosperous if Europe is to fight on indefinitely."

In *Bradstreet's Journal*, January 30, 1915, reference is made to the fact that in 1914 there were 16,769 business failures, the "largest number in the country's history." The following week this same journal called attention to the fact that "the largest number of business failures ever recorded in any month and the seventh largest monthly total of liabilities were noteworthy reports of the month of January." Two months later the picture was almost equally discouraging:—

April failures as reported numbered 1,691, a decrease of 10% from March, but an increase of 38% over April a year ago, and to this extent the largest total ever recorded in April.

It was the rapid growth of the munitions trade which rescued America from this serious economic situation. The value of explosives exported from the United States increased from $2,793,530 in March, 1915, to $32,197,274 in November of that year. Manufactures of iron and steel exported during the same period rose from $1,363,693 to $10,776,-183, while manufactures of brass mounted from $2,749,835 to $7,528,616.

It was only to be expected that the American Government should be exceedingly anxious to protect this trade that was reviving the drooping American industries. It was also obvious that the German Government would regard with growing concern these vast shipments of war supplies without which the Allied Powers would be in desperate straits. As early as February 14, 1915, Ambassador Gerard warned Secretary Bryan that German public opinion was so aroused over the American exports of munitions of war to the Allies that the situation was "very tense."

A month later Gerard sent a similar telegram to Secretary Bryan, in which he mentioned the bitter feeling engendered against America because of the munitions trade, and once again he informed the Department of State of the proximity of war:—

THREE WEEKS AGO, ALTHOUGH IT IS HARD FOR YOU IN AMERICA TO REALIZE IT, GERMANY WAS ON THE EDGE OF WAR WITH THE UNITED STATES AND THE GOVERNMENT HERE SEEMS BENT UPON AGAIN STIRRING UP TROUBLE.

On April 4, the German Ambassador left with Secretary Bryan a memorandum which indicated in very clear terms the position of the German Government in this matter of the export of war supplies from the United States to the Allied Governments. The general condition of affairs in the World War differed from

. . . that of any previous war. . . . In the present war all nations having a war material industry worth mentioning are either in-

volved in the war themselves or are engaged in perfecting their own armaments, and have therefore laid an embargo against the exportation of war material. The United States is accordingly the only neutral country in a position to furnish war materials. The conception of neutrality is thereby given a new purport, independently of the formal question of hitherto existing law. In contradiction thereto, the United States is building up a powerful arms industry in the broadest sense, the existing plants not only being worked but enlarged by all available means, and new ones built. . . . This industry is actually delivering goods only to the enemies of Germany. The theoretical willingness to supply Germany also, if shipments thither were possible, does not alter the case. If it is the will of the American people that there shall be a true neutrality, the United States will find means of preventing this one-sided supply of arms or at least of utilizing it to protect legitimate trade with Germany, especially that in foodstuffs.

Secretary Bryan waited more than two weeks before answering this memorandum from Ambassador Bernstorff. When he did so his note was couched in terms already familiar to the German Government. Any embargo upon the shipment of war materials from the United States would be "an unjustifiable departure from the principle of strict neutrality" which the American Government had consistently adhered to since the outbreak of the World War.

It is significant that Secretary Bryan failed to answer one of the most important items listed in the German memorandum of April 4, which referred to the fact that important European neutrals had laid embargoes upon the export of munitions of war. The American Government was constantly declaring that any embargo upon the export of munitions of war to the belligerent powers would be a violation of the principle of strict neutrality. The European neutrals had held a very different view and the Department of State seemed little interested in their attitude. It was not until August 30, 1915, that Secretary Lansing sent a circular telegram to American diplomatic officers in European neutral countries to request them to advise the Department of State with reference to the practice in the countries to which they were accredited. Answers were immediately forthcoming from the American representatives at Copenhagen, Stockholm, Christiania, Rome, The Hague, and Madrid to the effect that all these countries to which they were accredited had placed embargoes upon the export of arms and ammunition.

In commenting upon the action taken by these European neutral countries Secretary Lansing, in a letter to Mr. Tumulty, took occasion to remark as follows:—

Spain, Italy, Denmark, Sweden, Norway, and Holland prohibited the exportation of arms and ammunition in order, it is reported, to conserve their supplies for their own use. It is reported also that the exportation of such materials from any of these countries except possibly Italy, would, if allowed, have been of a negligible quantity. It is not possible to ascertain whether the real ground for the embargoes was, in some cases, that of conservation or really to avoid the enmity of the belligerents, to retaliate against some vexatious measure of the belligerents or to maintain a strict neutrality.

It is apparent, therefore, that the Department of State was fully advised that European neutral countries had placed embargoes upon the export of arms and ammunition soon after the outbreak of the World War. It is interesting to note, however, that Secretary Lansing did not request this information until the last days of August, 1915, and in the meantime the Secretary had prepared a final reply to the Central Powers concerning the exportation of American munitions of war. On June 29, 1915, the Austrian Minister of Foreign Affairs had addressed a long communication to Ambassador Penfield, protesting against the American trade in war munitions. When the Department of State received this communication it was forwarded at once to President Wilson, who suggested that "no categorical answer be made but that it be merely acknowledged." Secretary Lansing, however, did not accept this suggestion. To him the Austrian letter of June 29 appeared to offer an excellent opportunity for making a strong statement that would utterly confound both the Austrian Government and certain Americans who were in favor of embargoes upon the export of munitions— "Home consumption would be the real purpose; and answer to Austria the nominal purpose."

Having secured President Wilson's approval of a spirited letter to Austria, Secretary Lansing had Mr. Lester H. Woolsey, the Law Adviser to the Secretary of State, prepare an exhaustive study of the legal aspects of the munitions trade. Secretary Lansing himself made a careful examination of the practical aspects of the question, with emphasis upon the effect that embargo legislation would have upon a neutral nation like the United States. After completing a draft of the proposed reply to Austria, he sent it to President Wilson for advice. In his note of transmittal he adverted to the importance of a popular defense of the attitude of the Administration with regard to the export of war supplies:—

You will observe in reading it that it is presented in a popular rather than a technical manner because I think it will be more valuable for the public here in the United States than for its effect upon Austria-Hungary. . . . It is our first opportunity to present in a popular way the reasons why we should not restrict the exportation of munitions of war.

The reply of the President was somewhat disconcerting. The Chief Executive had read the proposed reply of Secretary Lansing most carefully, and the following questions immediately presented themselves:—

1. Can this argument not be taken as an argument in sympathy with the Allies and against militarism, which is Germany?

2. Are we not ourselves about to urge the control of the manufacture of arms and munitions by every government in our proposed understandings and undertakings with the Latin-American countries; and do we not wish ultimately to strive for the same thing in the final European settlement?

Of course, we are arguing only to the special case, and are absolutely unanswerable in our position that these things cannot be done *while a war is in progress* as against the parties to it; but how far, do you think, the arguments we urge in this paper will estop us in future deliberations on the peace and security of the world?

The argument in the proposed reply to which President Wilson took some exception was the one Secretary Lansing had prepared with respect to the effect that embargo legislation would have upon all neutrals in future wars. If a nation with a pacific background should become involved in war with a militaristic nation, a serious situation would result if all neutral nations refused to permit the shipment of arms to belligerents. The nation with a pacific background would not have the factories that could supply the requisite war materials, and unless it could import sufficient quantities of munitions from neutral nations it would soon be conquered by the militaristic nation that was adequately prepared for war.

In support of this argument he again wrote to President Wilson on August 6, and indicated the possible weakness of the stand of the Administration if it rested only upon a legal basis. It was possible that the legal argument would be sufficient to meet the contention of Austria, but it would not "satisfy the humanitarians." For this reason it seemed better to "insert the practical reason against prohibition and to show that it would compel general armament and so make for war rather than peace."

The President receded from his position, as he did in many instances when it came to a disagreement with Mr. Lansing, and on August 9 he approved the Lansing note with a few verbal changes. The instruction that was finally sent to Ambassador Penfield on August 12, 1915, was the definitive answer of the Administration to German and Austrian protests against the munitions trade. First, there was a long, legal argument in favor of the munitions trade. Next there was the *practical* argument which Secretary Lansing himself had prepared, and to which the President had raised some objections. It was summarized briefly:—

It has never been the policy of this country to maintain in time of peace a large military establishment or stores of arms and ammunition sufficient to repel invasion by a well-equipped and powerful enemy. . . . In consequence of this standing policy the United States would, in the event of attack by a foreign power, be at the outset of the war, seriously . . . embarrassed by the lack of arms and ammunition. . . . The United States has always depended upon the right and power to purchase arms and ammunition from neutral nations in case of foreign attack. This right, which it claims for itself, it can not deny to others.

This *practical* argument of which Secretary Lansing was so proud may have eased the consciences of certain American humanitarians, but it fell upon deaf German and Austrian ears. From the very beginning of the war the German press had sharply commented upon the fact that America was growing prosperous through a commerce that brought death and untold misery to countless Germans. This viewpoint is well expressed in the following excerpt from the German periodical *Kunstwart und Kulturwart*, in May, 1915:—

Are we actually fighting England, France and Russia, or are we in reality only fighting America? Hostile manufacturers state that everything depends upon the supply of munitions, and their supply would long since have become exhausted had America and Japan not assisted. Japan is a participant in the war. . . . But, America is neutral. . . . Let mockery, be it ever so bloody, be cast aside. In the final analysis it is capitalism and nothing else which is bringing this shame upon the United States. . . . If the honor of a state ever was on trial, it is surely the case with America today. As long as you Americans engage in selling munitions by the hundreds, yes, thousands and millions, which are being directed against the hearts of our brothers and sons, . . . so long to our ears will your prayers be but a mockery of God.

As the war continued and American munitions poured into England and France in ever increasing quantities, German sentiment towards America grew more and more bitter. Ambassador Gerard in his volume *My Four Years in Germany* frequently comments upon this feeling of hostility towards the United States which was created by the munitions trade. Even in court circles the sentiment against America was manifest:—

From the tenth of August 1914 to the twenty-fifth of September 1915, the Emperor continually refused to receive me on the ground that he would not receive the Ambassador of a country which furnished munitions to the enemies of Germany; and we were thoroughly blacklisted by all the German royalties.

In August, 1916, Ambassador Gerard reported a conversation with Gottlieb von Jagow, the German Secretary of State for Foreign Affairs, which clearly reflected the German attitude towards the American shipments of war supplies:—

He said that the offensive in the Somme could not continue without the great supply of shells from America. He also said that recently a German submarine submerged in the Channel had to allow forty-one ships to pass and that he was sure that each ship was full of ammunition and soldiers but probably had some American (?) also on board and therefore the submarine did not torpedo without warning. He seemed quite bitter.

This attitude of von Jagow is quite understandable when we look at the rising tide of munitions from America during the year 1916. The value of explosives exported from the United States had risen from $14,658,057 in August, 1915, to $74,925,413 in August, 1916. The value of exports of copper had increased during the same period from $7,781,487 to $20,319,053, while the exports of brass had mounted from $4,560,810 to $45,213,945. According to some authorities the total value of the exports of munitions during the calendar year 1916 reached the astounding figure of $1,290,000,000.

It is no wonder that as Germany became acquainted with the fact that America was supplying the most pressing needs of the Allied Governments at a time when every German need was denied because of the British blockade, the feeling throughout the Central Powers against the United States rose to new heights. A typical expression of this sentiment towards America may be seen in the following excerpt from a volume by Dr. Heinrich Pohl:—

Germany finds herself in the position of a warrior, hemmed in on all sides, whose enemies are all aiming at his heart. Every time this warrior succeeds in disarming the foe most harmful to him, every time the warrior strikes the sword from the hand of the enemy, a so-called neutral comes running from behind and places a new weapon in the hand of the defeated foe.

America, under the guise of neutrality, was serving the Allied Powers in a manner most suitable to their military plans against Germany. Even British publicists, who usually depreciate the contribution made by America to the Allied cause, have had to admit the decisive importance of the munitions trade, and Sir Edward Grey was frank enough to tell the real story of England's dependence upon American war supplies:—

Germany and Austria were self-supporting in the huge supply of munitions. The Allies soon became dependent for an adequate supply on the United States. If we quarrelled with the United States we could not get that supply. It was better, therefore, to carry on the war without blockade, if need be, than to incur a break with the United States about contraband and thereby deprive the Allies

of the resources necessary to carry on the war at all or with any chance of success.

To the German Government it appeared idle to talk of American neutrality in the face of this significant assistance to the Allied Powers. Moreover, it did seem that America was too prone to forget the attitude of the German Government towards the United States during the Spanish-American War. In 1898, the German Government, upon the request of the American Ambassador, searched a Spanish vessel suspected of carrying contraband from Hamburg to a Spanish port. Apparently, if this ship had been carrying contraband of war it would have been detained until this contraband cargo had been removed.

In 1914 the German Government had hardly hoped that America would follow this German precedent and refuse to permit the shipment of war supplies to the Allied Governments. As the munitions trade continued to grow, however, and it became apparent that America was serving as a base of war supplies that were necessary to Allied success, the German Government believed that this huge and decisive traffic was inconsistent with American neutrality. It was then that the German Government inclined towards the view that, in order to preserve an attitude of strict neutrality in America, the American Congress should be requested by President Wilson to give him the authority to impose an embargo upon the shipment of war supplies. In 1912, Congress had bestowed this authority upon the President with reference to the shipment of munitions to Mexico during the civil war then raging. In 1913 this war was still going on, and President Wilson, in a message to Congress in August of that year, had indicated his views as to the proper manner of preserving American neutrality:—

I deem it my duty to exercise the authority conferred upon me by the law of March 14, 1912, to see to it that neither side to this struggle now going on in Mexico receive any assistance from this side of the border. *I shall follow the best practice of nations in the matter of neutrality by forbidding the exportation of arms or munitions of war of any kind from the United States to any part of the Republic of Mexico.*

If in 1914 the President had followed "the best practice of nations in the matter of neutrality by forbidding the exportation of arms or munitions of war of any kind from the United States" it is very possible that America would not have been drawn into the World War. Before he could have proclaimed such an embargo against shipments of war materials to belligerent nations he would have had to secure the consent of Congress, but there had been no difficulty in persuading Congress to pass the necessary legislation when it came to stopping all exports of arms to Mexico. The industrial East would have fought vigorously against an embargo, but there was a strong pacifist sentiment in many sections of the United States which would have quickly rallied to the support of a restrictive policy. The President, however, never made the "slightest effort to obtain the legal authorization which would be required," and the traffic in munitions soon grew to such proportions that even had he been willing to take steps to curtail this trade it is more than doubtful whether Congress would have adopted his suggestion.

In January, 1916, Professor Charles C. Hyde, one of America's foremost authorities in the field of international law, wrote to Secretary Lansing regarding the dangers involved in the munitions trade. It was apparent to him that the American Government might have to place an embargo upon the export of war materials, and he believed that such action could safely be taken on the ground that Great Britain had refused to heed American protests against unlawful restrictions imposed upon American commerce, or upon the ground that the unrestricted exportation of arms to the Allied Governments would cause Germany to "take steps both hostile and injurious to the United States."

Under existing conditions, the United States was becoming a "base of supplies of such magnitude that unless retarded, the success of armies, possibly the fate of empires, may ultimately rest upon the output of American factories." Such a decisive rôle would inevitably lead America to become "a party to the conflict." This being so, it behooved America to study most carefully the course it should take with reference to the export of arms. There was little doubt that from a strictly legal viewpoint this trade in munitions of war had many precedents in its favor, but it was somewhat questionable whether this mere legal right as a neutral,

. . . to sell war material to a belligerent state to enable it to cripple an adversary with which the United States is at peace, would . . . appeal to the American people to a degree such that they would consent to make war for the mere purpose of preserving that commercial privilege.

The reply of Secretary Lansing to this letter of friendly warning concerning the obvious implications of the munitions trade is not available to scholars at the present time, but from his acrid notes to Germany and to Austria-Hungary, and from the frank revelations in his *War Memoirs* it is not difficult to imagine the indifferent attitude he assumed towards such a communication. War, and not peace, was his desire. From the moment he became Secretary of State he looked forward to a conflict between the United States and Germany as a necessary incident in the crusade against German militarism. With this idea constantly in mind he was in no mood to listen to suggestions that the exports of American munitions be curtailed. He firmly believed that the Allied Governments should be given all the assistance that was possible under a most liberal interpretation of American neutrality.

America was already well advanced on the road to war, and she was not to be checked by the weak barriers of neutral obligations.

. . . One of the chief complaints voiced by the business world against the Wilson Administration was the fact that both the President and the Secretary of State had informed the big banking interests of their opposition to the extensions of loans to the belligerent powers. This action was merely one phase of their general attitude of opposition towards the practices of "economic imperialism" which in world politics had placed the weak nations at the mercy of strong, capitalistic nations like Great Britain, France, and Germany. As early as March, 1913, the Administration had displeased the bankers by the adverse position it took with reference to the six-power consortium loan to China, and in 1914 there was to be further friction. The outbreak of the World War created many problems of international finance, and Secretary Bryan was fearful that

American loans to belligerent powers would influence banking groups to become partisans of the nations to whom they loaned their money. If neutrality were to be the watchword of the Administration it was essential to overlook no means of preserving it.

As the Secretary had anticipated, the large banking interests were deeply interested in the World War because of wide opportunities for large profits. On August 3, 1914, even before the actual clash of arms, the French firm of Rothschild Frères cabled to Morgan and Company in New York suggesting the flotation of a loan of $100,000,000, a substantial part of which was to be left in the United States to pay for French purchases of American goods.

On the following day Morgan and Company sent an answering cable to the Rothschilds expressing regret that the situation in America made it impossible to float such a loan. Such conditions, however, were probably only temporary, and after a little while it

. . . might be very possible and excellent thing to do and shall hope to take up question with you soon as possible.

A few days later Herman Harjes, the Morgan representative in Paris, inquired as to the establishment of French credits in the United States. Mr. Harjes admitted that he was "most desirous" to do everything possible for the French Government, and suggested that if a large loan could not be raised in the United States it might be possible to make credit arrangements for at least $10,000,000 on the basis of French Treasury bills. On August 11, Mr. Harjes again cabled to Morgan and Company and anxiously pressed for a loan as large as $20,000,000 against

French one-year Treasury bills. This loan was to be used exclusively for purchases of American goods, and would not in any way withdraw gold from the United States.

In the face of these cablegrams from the Rothschilds and from Mr. Harjes, Morgan and Company inquired of the Department of State as to its attitude towards credit arrangements for certain belligerent powers. Secretary Bryan's response was immediate and negative. In a letter to President Wilson, August 10, 1914, he outlined his principal objections to any effort on the part of belligerent nations to float loans in the United States. First of all, he "knew nothing that would do more to prevent wars than an international agreement that neutral nations would not loan to belligerents." The United States was "the one great nation which is not involved and our refusal to loan to any belligerents would naturally tend to hasten a conclusion of the war." Moreover, if the United States

. . . approved of a loan to France we could not, of course, object to a loan to Great Britian, Germany, Russia, Austria or to any other country, and if loans were made to these countries our citizens would be divided into groups, each group loaning money to the country which it favors and this money could not be furnished without expressions of sympathy. These expressions of sympathy are disturbing enough when they do not rest upon pecuniary interests—they would be still more disturbing if each group was pecuniarily interested in the success of the nation to whom its members had loaned money.

Finally, Secretary Bryan prophesied what would happen if banking groups in the United States were permitted to underwrite loans to any of the belligerent nations. As soon as these loans were successfully floated,

. . . the powerful financial interests which would be connected with these loans would be tempted to use their influence through the newspapers to support the interest of the Government to which they had loaned because the value of the security would be directly affected by the result of the war. . . . All of this influence would make it all the more difficult for us to maintain neutrality, as our action on various questions that would arise would affect one side or the other and powerful financial interests would be thrown into the balance.

In a postscript to this letter Secretary Bryan further called the attention of the President to a statement made by Mr. Lansing to the effect that "an American citizen who goes abroad and voluntarily enlists in the army of a belligerent nation loses the protection of his citizenship while so engaged." This being so, Mr. Lansing had asked

. . . why dollars going abroad and enlisting in the war, should be more protected?

In commenting upon this question propounded by Mr. Lansing, Secretary Bryan concluded as follows:—

As we cannot prevent American citizens going abroad at their own risk, so we cannot prevent dollars going abroad at the risk of the owners, but the influence of the Government is used to prevent American citizens from doing this. Would the Government not be justified in using its influence against the enlistment of the nation's dollars in a foreign war?

In this instance the Secretary of State possessed the hermetic gift of putting wings to words—words that flew so close to the President's heart that he pinned the following memorandum to the Secretary's letter:—

In the judgment of this government loans by American bankers to any foreign government which is at war is inconsistent with the true spirit of neutrality.

At one o'clock in the afternoon of August 10, Secretary Bryan talked over the long-distance telephone with Mr. Davison, of Morgan and Company, and indicated to him some of the objections which the Department of State had with regard to making loans to belligerents. After this conversation, Morgan and Company cabled to Mr. Harjes that it was doing its "very best" to arrange credits for the French Government, and that it ardently desired to be "of service." Although there were no legal objections to such a loan, yet in view of the "present strained circumstances" it was deemed expedient not to take any action that might be "offensive" to the Administration.

After having secured the assent of the President to a policy of nonextension of loans to belligerent powers, Secretary Bryan, on August 15, sent the following telegram to Morgan and Company:—

THERE IS NO REASON WHY LOANS SHOULD NOT BE MADE TO THE GOVERNMENTS OF NEUTRAL NATIONS, BUT IN THE JUDGMENT OF THIS GOVERNMENT, LOANS BY AMERICAN BANKERS TO ANY FOREIGN NATION WHICH IS AT WAR ARE INCONSISTENT WITH THE TRUE SPIRIT OF NEUTRALITY.

The House of Morgan was too astute to press the issue any further at that moment, so they reluctantly cabled to Harjes, in Paris, that owing to the adverse attitude of the American Government they were unable to "negotiate loan to French Government."

It was apparent that Morgan and Company was very anxious to preserve harmonious relations with the Wilson Administration, and according to Mr. Thomas W. Lamont, "every move of the firm in those harried days was made only after consultation with the Department of State." When Mr. Lamont was asked by Senator Nye [in 1936] if he had been the intermediary between the House of Morgan and the Department of State he at once became noncommittal: "I do not swear I did not, but it was more than twenty years ago." Mr. Morgan himself was equally uncertain: "It might have been me, but if so I have no recollection that it was."

The unsympathetic stand taken by Secretary Bryan relative to the extension of loans to belligerents prevented for the time being any action by Morgan and Company, but it did not long deter Mr. Frank A. Vanderlip, President of the National City Bank, from perfecting certain credit arrangements for the French Government. Mr. Vanderlip has proudly admitted that from the very moment Germany invaded Belgium he was "wholeheartedly for the Allies." He was "glad to do anything he could for France," and because of this friendly attitude he wrote to the French Ambassador, Jules Jusserand, to offer his assistance. It was the opinion of his bank that

. . . at the present time $10,000,000 one-year Treasury warrants could be sold in the United States on a 6 per cent. basis, not to the public, but to large institutions to whom an appeal could be made on other than strictly investment lines. This would be on the condition however, that the transaction is not objected to by our Government at Washington, and that the proceeds of these securities remain on deposit . . . until expended exclusively for products of the United States.

After this indication of his friendly feeling for France, Mr. Vanderlip then made a gesture that was worthy of Chevalier Bayard at his best:—

As I have explained before, we do not want and do not intend to keep any commission on this transaction. . . . This bank desires to render this service to your Government freely and without any special compensation.

M. Jusserand must have been overwhelmed at such generosity, but he recovered in time to write to Mr. Vanderlip on October 14, and after expressing his appreciation of such financial knight-errantry, he concluded with the ardent hope that "this first operation . . . is the beginning of more important ones in the near future." Needless to say, the French Government accepted the proposal "with great pleasure."

The main difficulty in the way of an extension of credit to the French Government was the position taken by Secretary Bryan on August 15 with reference to loans to belligerent nations. But this position was apparently so vulnerable to attacks from "big business" that it had to be partially abandoned in mid-October. In the early part of that month Mr. Vanderlip sent one of the officials of the National City Bank to Washington to discuss the financial situation with Secretary Bryan. The Secretary was soon overcome by a barrage of technical terms and consented to a compromise which was in essence a "strategic retreat" from the position he held on August 15. On October 15 the Department of State issued a press release to the effect that the President possessed no legal authority to interfere in any way with the trade between the people of the United States and the nationals of belligerent countries.

Along with this press release there were certain "inspired" articles in the New York papers which explained the new attitude taken by the Department of State. According to the New York *Times* (October 16), it was admitted

. . . in a high authoritative quarter today that shipments of gold to belligerent countries and loans by American bankers to bankers or other persons in belligerent countries were to be regarded as included in the shipments of contraband articles. . . . It was explained that there was a distinction between loans made by the Government of the United States to belligerent governments and loans made by individual citizens.

In the New York *World* (October 16) it was stated that the President had prevented J. P. Morgan and other big bankers from granting a loan to France merely by persuasion and "not by reference to any power possessed by the Chief Executive." In the *Annalist* the press release of the Department of State was interpreted to mean that "the Government has now definitely ruled that American bankers may make loans to bankers or other persons in belligerent countries."

There was no attempt on the part of officials in the Department of State to correct these interpretative statements in the New York press, which were soon regarded as authentic. But the banking world wished to have assurances from the President himself, and for this reason Mr. Vanderlip instructed one of the vice-presidents of the National City Bank to write a shrewd letter to Mr. Lansing. After pointing out how the World War had seriously obstructed the ordinary channels of commerce, this bank official then indicated the best mode of removing these barriers. It was necessary to grant certain belligerent powers like England, France, and Russia temporary credits lest the

. . . buying power of these foreign purchasers will go to Australia, Canada, Argentina and elsewhere. . . . If we allow these purchases to go elsewhere we will have neglected our foreign trade at the time of our greatest need and greatest opportunity.

In order to meet this pressing need the National City Bank was especially anxious to

. . . grant short-time banking credits to European governments, both belligerent and neutral, and where necessary or desirable, replenish their cash balance on this side by the purchase of short-time Treasury warrants. Such purchases would necessarily be limited to the legal capacity of the bank, and as these warrants are bearer warrants without interest, they could not and would not be made the subject of a public issue.

This letter from one of the vice-presidents of the National City Bank to Mr. Lansing was written for the purpose of confirming in the mind of the Counselor of the Department of State the many points that had been discussed during the course of a conversation between Mr. Lansing and Mr. Samuel McRoberts on the morning of October 23. It is barely possible that Mr. McRoberts, as one of the vice-presidents of the National City Bank, was the author of this letter from which we have just quoted. In that case he probably handed this letter to Mr. Lansing shortly after the termination of their conference. Mr. Lansing then hurried to the Department of State, where he hastily prepared a memorandum entitled "Summary of Information in Regard to Credits of Foreign Governments in This Country and the Relation to Trade." In this memorandum Mr. Lansing made no effort to digest and paraphrase the suggestions contained in the bank official's letter to

him. Instead, he merely copied verbatim the phraseology of the letter that had been handed to him and only inserted an occasional "I" to make it appear as though these suggestions were his own. That evening he paid a visit to the White House and submitted the memorandum to President Wilson.

Inasmuch as Secretary Bryan was out of the city there was no opportunity to secure his views. Neither the President nor the Counselor was familiar with the complicated mechanism of international trade, but there is no record that they sought the assistance of any of the experts in the Treasury Department. Because of his enlightening conversation with Mr. McRoberts it is possible that Mr. Lansing felt competent to handle the situation. Moreover, he had the hastily manufactured memorandum based upon the letter from the official in the National City Bank, and armed with this data he probably thought he would have little difficulty in impressing the President with his apparent grasp of international finance.

The conference between the President and Mr. Lansing was short and decisive. After Mr. Lansing's memorandum had been carefully read and commented upon, the Chief Executive immediately took his proper cue and recited the following lines to the Counselor:—

There is a decided difference between an issue of government bonds, which are sold in open market to investors, and an arrangement for easy exchange in meeting debts incurred in trade between a government and American merchants. The sale of bonds draws gold from the American people. The purchasers of bonds are loaning their savings to the belligerent government, and are, in fact, financing the war. The acceptance of Treasury notes or other evidences of debt in payment for articles purchased in this country is merely a means of facilitating trade by a system of credits which will avoid the clumsy and impracticable method of cash payments. . . . The question of an arrangement of this sort ought not to be submitted to this government for its opinion, since it has given its views on loans in general, although an arrangement as to credits has to do with a commercial debt rather than with a loan of money.

This inspired decision of the President clearly indicates how important banking interests were using Mr. Lansing as a mouthpiece of their propaganda. It also shows that Mr. Lansing had far more influence with the President than is generally believed. In this case the decision of the President marked a distinct change in the attitude of the Administration towards "big business," and it "involved a recession from a position based upon 'the true spirit of neutrality' to one based upon 'strict legality.' "

On the evening of October 24, Mr. Lansing met Willard Straight at the Metropolitan Club, in Washington, and promptly informed him of the favorable disposition of the President with reference to the acceptance by American bankers of the Treasury notes of certain belligerent nations. It was certainly unusual for the Acting Secretary of State to divulge to a mere acquaintance such confidential information, and his action takes on increasing significance when it is remembered that Mr. Straight had for many years been closely associated with the House of Morgan and was at that time actually in their employ. Apparently, Mr. Lansing was on terms of intimacy with certain agents of Wall Street, and his subsequent strong advocacy of large loans to belligerent nations is not surprising.

It is possible that on this occasion Mr. Lansing was more loquacious than usual, and it might well be that he did not confine his confidential utterances to the receptive ears of Mr. Straight. Perhaps Mr. Straight himself told certain friends of this conference with the Counselor of the Department of State. At any rate we find that on October 25, the day after the Lansing-Straight conference, Ambassador Jusserand wrote the following letter to Mr. Samuel McRoberts, of the National City Bank:—

I think it is appropriate for me to confidentially tell you from information, the accuracy of which I cannot doubt, [that] you will find the competent authorities [Wilson-Lansing-McAdoo] ready, not of course to grant a "permission" which is neither asked for nor wanted, but to abstain from objections.

Upon the receipt of this reassuring news the National City Bank announced in the New York *Times* (October 30, 1914) that arrangements were being completed to extend to the French Government a special credit of $10,000,000. Official notice of this arrangement was sent out on November 4, and the cornerstone of the vast structure of American financial aid to the Allies was thus formally laid. . . .

The real reasons why America went to war cannot be found in any single set of circumstances. There was no clear-cut road to war that the President followed with certain steps that knew no hesitation. There were many dim trails of doubtful promise, and one along which he traveled with early misgivings and reluctant tread was that which led to American economic solidarity with the Allies.

PAUL BIRDSALL's (1899–   ) version of the role of economic factors is at once more sophisticated and more determinist than that of either Tansill or the Nye Committee. Birdsall, who also wrote *Versailles Twenty Years After* (1941), a strongly pro-Wilson study of the peace negotiations, argues in the review essay reprinted here that the need to maintain domestic prosperity rather than the influence of bankers persuaded the Wilson administration to approve the private loans which financed the war trade. As that trade mounted Germany, believing that the United States could hardly be of more harm in the war than out, made its decision to resort to the submarine campaign.*

Neutrality and Economic Pressures

Twenty years of debate have not yet produced a satisfactory or even a coherent neutrality policy for the United States, nor have they yet offered any real understanding of the problem of neutrality in the modern world to serve as a basis for policy making. Until we have some adequate analysis of the forces which destroyed President Wilson's neutrality policy between 1914 and 1917 no government is likely to be more successful than his in future efforts to master such forces. Nor will the neutrality legislation of the past years help very much if it simply ignores these forces.

The trouble with much of the writing on the World War period is that it deals with separate aspects of the problem in watertight compartments with complete disregard of the complex interrelations between economic and political phenomena. Thus Charles Seymour deals almost exclusively with the diplomatic record of our relations with Imperial Germany and from that record draws the only possible conclusion, that "It was the German submarine warfare and nothing else that forced him [Wilson] to lead America into war." The late Newton D. Baker arrives by the same route at the same conclusion: "Certainly the occasion of the United States entering the World War was the resumption of submarine warfare." That Baker had

* Paul Birdsall, "Neutrality and Economic Pressures, 1914–1917," *Science and Society*, III (Spring, 1939), pp. 217–228. Reprinted without footnotes by permission of Science and Society, Inc.

a glimpse of more remote and subtile causation is indicated by his choice of the word "occasion" and by his admission that critics may with some justification charge him with oversimplification by confusing "occasion" with "cause." "This," he says, "I may to some extent have done." Each of these authors is content with a surface record of diplomacy and politics without reference to the fundamental context of economic and social phenomena which alone can give it significance for analysis of the large problem of neutrality.

Nor does it advance the investigation to turn one's back completely on the diplomatic record and resort to a narrow economic determinism, as does Senator Nye. Ignoring the inescapable evidence that German submarine warfare was the immediate "occasion" for American entry into the war, he argues the simple thesis that American bankers first forced the American Government to authorize large loans to France and Great Britain, and when those countries were faced with defeat, then forced the American Government into the war to protect the bankers' investments. I have heard Senator Nye publicly express embarrassment at the lack of any direct evidence to support the second, and for his purposes the essential, part of his thesis, but what he lacks in evidence he makes up in faith.

What is most needed is careful synthesis of the accurate and valid parts of the diplomatic and economic theses. Senator Nye's committee has given us invaluable data on the development of close economic ties with the Entente Powers in the face of a government policy of neutrality designed to prevent just that development, even if the committee failed to analyze the precise forces at work. We have accurate and scholarly studies explaining the *immediate* cause of American intervention as due to the German decision to wage unrestricted submarine warfare. But no one has yet demonstrated the connection between American economic ties with Germany's enemies and Germany's submarine campaign which provoked American intervention. It is precisely this connection which reveals the true significance of the economic relationship, namely that it makes neutrality in modern war impossible—unless the economic relationships with belligerents can somehow be prevented. And that must be the first subject of investigation.

II

If Senator Nye is right in contending that it was primarily the intrigues of the banking interests which prevented a genuine neutrality policy, then the present legislation[1] to curb such activity in the future should prove adequate. But careful study of the evidence he has himself unearthed does not bear him out.

The Wilson administration attempted to enforce a neutrality policy identical with that now prescribed by statute in respect to loans to belligerents. To be sure there was no effort to prevent the sale of munitions to belligerents, and Secretary of State Bryan explained why in a letter of January 20, 1915 to Senator Stone of the Senate Committee on Foreign Relations. He said that "the duty of a neutral to restrict trade in munitions of war has never been imposed by international law or municipal statute. . . . [It] has never been the policy of this government to prevent the ship-

[1] Written in 1939, this refers to the neutrality act of 1937.—Ed.

ment of arms or ammunition into belligerent territory, except in the case of the American Republics, and then only when civil strife prevailed." Moreover the German government admitted the legality of the munitions traffic as late as December 15, 1914 even while they complained of its disadvantage to their cause.

Very different was the official attitude toward loans to belligerent governments. The State Department recognized no greater legal obligation to prevent them than the sale of munitions. Lansing, Bryan's subordinate and successor, said he knew of no legal objection but agreed with Bryan in urging that the United States government refuse to approve loans to belligerents. Bryan said that "money is the worst of all contrabands," and on August 15, 1914, wrote J. P. Morgan, who wished to finance a French loan, "There is no reason why loans should not be made to the governments of neutral nations, but in the judgment of this government, *loans by American bankers to any foreign nation which is at war are inconsistent with the spirit of true neutrality.*" Our State Department has never received the credit it deserves for its realistic appraisal of the issues of neutrality and its refusal to take refuge in the technicalities of international law. It is scarcely the fault of the State Department that powerful economic forces almost at once began to undermine its policy and within the year forced its abandonment. Nor can it be denied that the German government itself helped destroy the policy by sinking the *Lusitania.*

The first efforts to modify the State Department's policy came from the bankers, specifically the house of J. P. Morgan. Lamont testifies that Morgan's

firm accepted the State Department ruling but asked permission at least to extend credits to foreign governments to facilitate purchases in the United States, on the theory that this was purely a bookkeeping arrangement very different from the sale of belligerent bonds on the open market. On October 23, 1914 Lansing recorded a conversation he had with President Wilson dealing with this request, in which Wilson accepted the distinction as valid. "There is a decided difference between an issue of government bonds, sold in the open market to investors, and an arrangement for easy exchange in meeting debts incurred between the government and American merchants." The latter was merely a means of facilitating trade. Accordingly Straight of the firm of Morgan was authorized to open credits of this character for belligerent governments, particularly the French. On March 31, 1915 the State Department issued a public statement of its policy in the following press release. "While loans to belligerents have been disapproved, this government has not felt that it was justified in interposing objections to the credit arrangements which have been brought to its attention. It has neither approved these nor disapproved—it has simply taken no action and expressed no opinion."

The destruction of the *Lusitania* by a German submarine undermined the State Department's neutrality policy in two ways, by causing the resignation of Bryan (who refused to take responsibility for Wilson's stiff notes of protest to Germany), and by establishing in the post of Secretary of State his former subordinate Lansing. Lansing says in his memoirs that after the *Lusitania* there was always in his mind the "conviction that we would ultimately become the ally of Britain." He was therefore less disposed to maintain the rigid standards of neutrality set by Bryan. Yet in the event it was economic pressures that overwhelmed the policy.

In August of 1915 the British pound sterling began to sag in the exchange market under the pressure of war finance, and the first note of warning of threat to American export business appears in a letter of August 14 from Governor Strong of the New York Federal Reserve Bank to Col. House. Strong said that the drop of sterling to below $4.71 had already led to cancellation of many foreign contracts for the purchase of American grain. He predicted more to follow and feared for the drastic curtailment of all American exports. On August 21 Secretary of the Treasury McAdoo wrote to President Wilson, "Great Britain is and always has been our best customer. . . . The high prices for food products have brought great prosperity to the farmers, while the purchasers of war munitions have stimulated industry and have set factories going to full capacity. . . . Great prosperity is coming. It is, in large measure, already here. It will be tremendously increased if we can extend reasonable credits to our customers." It was therefore imperative, he said, that Great Britain be permitted to float a loan of $500,000,000 at once. "To maintain our prosperity we must finance it." Unfortunately, according to him, the way was barred by the State Department ban on foreign loans, and by the pro-German attitude of two members of the Federal Reserve Board, Miller and Warburg.

Wilson's reply was an evasion. On August 26, he wrote Lansing, "My opinion is that we should say that 'parties would take no action either for or against such a transaction,' but that this should be orally conveyed, and not put in writing. Yrs. W. W." But Lansing wanted something more definite and wrote a long letter rehearsing all McAdoo's arguments. "Doubtless Sec'y McAdoo has discussed with you the necessity of floating government loans for the belligerent nations, which are purchasing such great quantities of goods in this country, in order to avoid a serious financial situation which will not only affect them but this country as well." He estimated excess of American exports over imports for the entire year at $2,500,000,000 and alleged that the figure from December 1, 1914 to June 30, 1915 was only slightly less than $1,000,000,000. "If the European countries cannot find the means to pay for the excess of goods sold them over those purchased from them, they will have to stop buying and our present export trade will shrink proportionately. The result would be restriction of output, industrial depression, idle capital, idle labor, numerous failures, financial demoralization, and general unrest and suffering among the laboring classes. . . . Can we afford to let a declaration as to our conception of the 'true spirit of neutrality,' made in the early days of the war, stand in the way of our national interests which seem to be seriously threatened?" McAdoo had stressed the opportunity for national prosperity; Lansing threatened the horrors of national depression. Wilson replied two days later, on September 8, "I have no doubt that our oral discussion of this letter suffices. If it does not, will you let me know that you would like a written reply? W. W." Shortly after this the house of Morgan floated a loan of $500,000,000 on behalf of the British and French governments.

What of Senator Nye's contention that the bankers got us into thè war by exerting direct pressure on Washington to protect their "investment"? It remains to be proved that the investment did get us into the war, and it is perfectly clear that direct pressure on Washington ceased when their desire to float loans for belligerent governments was granted. It is likewise clear that the government did not relinquish its ban on such loans out of any tender concern for the bankers as a group. What McAdoo, Lansing, and Wilson feared was a national economic depression. The bankers were in the happy position of being able to serve both God and Mammon. The situation is summarized in a single paragraph of Lansing's letter of September 6: "I believe that Secretary McAdoo is convinced, and I agree with him, that there is only one means of avoiding this situation which would so seriously affect economic conditions in this country, and that is the flotation of large bond issues by the belligerent governments. Our financial institutions have the money to loan and wish to do so."

At this point the conclusions of Seymour and Baker seem irresistible. They conclusively demonstrate from the diplomatic record that German resort to unrestricted submarine warfare was the immediate cause of American participation in the war. Yet they are strangely incurious about the reasons for the German decision, which have a very direct connection with the American departure from its own deliberately adopted policy of forbidding loans to belligerents. The fact that the German decision was made with full realization that it would force the United States into the war is certainly something that needs to be explained and the search for an explanation is revealing.

III

There were two forces struggling for control within Germany, the civilian government of Chancellor Bethmann-Hollweg, and the naval-military element. The latter favored extreme military policies without regard to diplomatic consequences, while Bethmann waged a losing fight on behalf of elementary political common-sense. In regard to the specific issue of submarine warfare the military group were uncompromising advocates of its unrestricted use as against Bethmann's warnings that such a policy was certain to bring the United States into the war in the ranks of Germany's enemies. After the sinking of the *Sussex* in March 1916 Bethmann was able to dominate the situation for the rest of the year. On May 4, 1916 the German Government gave to the United States a pledge to abide by the rules of cruiser warfare, abandoning the attacks on passenger ships, and promising to obey the rules of visit and search as they applied to merchant vessels. That the pledge was conditional on American enforcement of international law on Great Britain was a clear indication that Bethmann's victory was not decisive. The military element opposed the pledge from the beginning and fought for its abrogation from May throughout the rest of the year, with ultimate success.

They did not in the least contest the civilian thesis that unrestricted submarine warfare would force the United States into the war. They blithely admitted it—and said it did not matter! Here is the reasoning. On May 4, the very day of the *Sussex* pledge, General Falkenhayn wrote Bethmann: "I consider unrestricted U-boat warfare not only one, but the *only* effective instrument of war at our disposal capable of bringing England to consider peace negotiations. . . . So far as this situation is concerned [the probable entry of the United States into the war] *America's step from secret war in which it has long been engaged against us, to an openly declared hostility can effect no real change.*" Hindenburg and Ludendorff grew more and more impatient of the civilians' incurable timidity about war with the United States. They renewed their attack at the end of August, and Holtzendorff of the Admiralty Staff carried their complaints to Bethmann. "The objections to this mode of warfare are not considered mainly from the standpoint of the effect upon England, but from that of the reaction upon the United States. . . . *The United States can scarcely engage in more hostile activities than she has already done up to this time.*" On August 31 at Pless, the civilian and military elements fought it out, with Jagow, Helferrich, and Bethmann standing firmly together against the generals. All three warned that war with the United States must inevitably follow resumption of submarine warfare, and that active American participation would be fatal to Germany. For the time being they again won their point, and it was agreed that final decision might await the outcome of the Rumanian campaign. Even after that Bethmann was permitted to try his hand at peace negotiations in December, but their complete failure, coupled with Wilson's inability to mediate, inevitably brought renewed pressure from the military. Ludendorff on December 22 told the Foreign Office again that formal American participation in the war would alter nothing, and on the same day Holtzendorff brought in an Admiralty report to much the same effect. It dismissed the danger of American troops by showing how much time was needed for their training and transport; it calculated that the American supply of munitions—already at capacity—would be less rather than more available to Germany's enemies because they would be reserved for American use. Positive advantage would accrue to Germany from restored freedom of action in sinking even passenger ships which carried munitions. The only disadvantage conceded by the report was the possible increase in American loans to the belligerents, but the amount of these was already so tremendous a factor in the economic strength of the hostile coalition that little additional danger from that source was to be anticipated. Bethmann had for some time been yielding to the arguments and the importunities of the military, and the conference at Pless on January 9, 1917 sealed his defeat by the decision to renew unrestricted submarine warfare. Hindenburg's final words were, "It simply must be. We are counting on the possibility of war with the United States, and have made all preparations to meet it. *Things cannot be worse than they now are.* The war must be brought to an end by the use of all means as soon as possible." The United States declared war on April 6, 1917.

The civilians were right and the military were wrong in their calculations as to the ultimate importance of a formal declaration of war by the United States. But the arguments of the military were plausible and they carried the day. Their promise to reduce England speedily to prostration was tempting, but it was essentially a gamble, and it is hard to see how they could have overborne civilian opposition if they had not had so plausible an answer to the one serious argument that the civilians presented. The answer was always that formal participation of the United States in the war would bring no change in the fundamental situation of American economic support to the Allies. The major influence in shaping the decision which brought the United States into the war is to be found in American policy in the economic sphere, specifically the decision of the Wilson administration in August, 1915 to abandon a policy deliberately adopted in the interest of neutrality early in the war. It was government permission to bankers to float loans for belligerent governments in order to finance American export trade that provided the Allies with resources which Germany could not obtain. That in turn weighted the scales in favor of the extremists and against the moderates in Germany, and provoked the decision which forced the United States into the war.

It is equally clear that the administration yielded to pressures which no administration is likely to withstand. The alternative policy of strict adherence to its earlier standards of neutrality meant economic depression on a national scale. It is scarcely drawing the long bow to say that the fundamental cause of the failure of American neutrality policy was economic, nor is it unreasonable to suppose that the same economic factors will again in the future make a genuine and strict policy of neutrality unworkable, no matter what laws may be written on the statute books to enforce it. The only sensible course is to renounce our illusions and to face the world of reality where there is no longer any such thing as neutrality. In the face of a possible collapse of the collective security system as an alternative to ostrich isolationism

and "neutrality" the area of choice is tragically narrowed. It would seem to involve a choice between deciding whether we should now affirm our decision publicly that we will align ourselves with the democracies of the world in the event of war on the long chance of preventing the war, or follow that policy of drift which will sooner or later involve us in inevitable war without our having any very clear cut program of war aims to achieve.

IV

Is such realism conceivable in the present state of confusion of mind? Probably not, because of the tenacity of outworn but hallowed concepts and policies. Neutrality has a long history and its own particular folklore. Two of its high priests, Borchard and Lage, treat it as an all-sufficient decalogue when rightly interpreted and strictly adhered to. ". . . Neutral rights were as clear in 1914 as was any other branch of public law, and while the law was grossly violated during the war, it has not thereby been ended or modified." The real difficulty they discover in Wilson's repudiation of "the very basis of American tradition in foreign policy." The submarine controversy with Germany is made to turn on Wilson's "insistence as a matter of National Honor that American citizens were priviliged to travel unmolested on belligerent vessels." It follows that there was no adequate excuse for the United States to break "with its fundamental principles by the unprecedented decision to participate in a European war. . . ." Consequently there is no need to explore the economic background against which the drama of neutrality was played out, unless indeed there was no such drama at all, but only a skillful bit of play acting. Borchard and Lage devote exactly one page out of a total of three hundred and fifty to the administration's retreat from its original prohibition of loans to belligerent governments, with the remark that "No more than casual reference needs to be made to one of the more egregious lurches into unneutrality, whereby the United States and its people were led into financing the munitions supply of one set of the belligerents, the Allies." In their account this appears as but a minor detail in a general policy of partisanship of the Allies' cause. And so at the end they reject the argument that the conditions of the modern world make American neutrality impossible as "humiliating to American independence." Denying the efficacy of any improvised formula, they recommend "an honest intention to remain aloof from foreign conflict, a refusal to be stampeded by unneutral propaganda, *a knowledge of the law and capacity to stand upon it,* meeting emergencies and problems not romantically but wisely." It can be argued plausibly that President Wilson fought against overwhelming odds to realize exactly that program.

At least historians should not become victims of the legal exegesis that obscures the unreality of the neutrality concept. But the latest and most comprehensive account of American intervention in the World War, Tansill's *America Goes to War,* is almost totally lacking in interpretative treatment and completely lacking in synthesis. His very full chapters on the events leading to abandonment of the administration's loan policy are written largely in terms of "War Profits Beckon to 'Big Business,' " with very little reference to the administration's concern with the economic condition of the country as a whole. Moreover he fails completely to show the political and diplomatic implications of the economic ties in his concluding paragraph that deals with them. "The real reasons why America went to war cannot be found in any single set of circumstances. There was no clear-cut road to war that the President followed with certain steps that knew no hesitation. There were many dim trails of doubtful promise, and one along which he travelled with early misgivings and reluctant tread was that which led to American economic solidarity with the Allies." Tansill leaves it at that without any attempt to pursue the profound effect of this economic solidarity on the equilibrium of political forces in Germany which I have been at pains to trace in the central portion of this essay. This is all the more remarkable because Tansill is the only writer on the subject who has conscientiously studied that unstable equilibrium extensively in the German official documents. He has used most if not all of the documents I have cited to prove the decisive effect of the economic argument on the submarine decision—and many more—without ever apparently noting the presence of that argument at all. In his quotations from the documents he simply does not quote the passages where the argument appears. Despite his failure to see relationships, and his avoidance of interpretation, his account is still the fullest treatment available of all the complex phenomena, economic, political, psychological, inherent in the neutrality problem. But it is a compendium devoid of significance for an intelligent understanding of the neutrality problem.

The definitive study at once analytical and interpretative as well as comprehensive has yet to appear, and until it does appear there is small hope of enlightenment.

The selections presented thus far were written
before World War II; all but one of those that
follow were written after, a fact which in large
measure accounts for their different perspective and
assumptions. An example is this selection from
Woodrow Wilson and the Balance of Power (1955) by
EDWARD H. BUEHRIG (1910–   ), which takes
issue with Tansill, the Nye Committee, and Birdsall
in their respective versions of the economic argument.
In its place Buehrig, an Indiana University professor
of international relations and author of several essays on
Wilsonian diplomacy, introduces considerations of
"balance of power" and "security," concepts with which
the earlier students of American involvement were
￾arely concerned. This selection might profitably be
re-read later along with Walter Lippmann's article
on the security thesis.*

The Economic Motive Challenged

It is a relatively simple matter to
understand the purpose of Germany's
submarine policy. In part it was supple-
mentary to the fighting on land, designed
to hamper the supply of Allied armies.
It had also a second objective: so decisive a defeat of Great Britain as to
end her traditional control of the seas.
The latter objective was uppermost in
the decision for waging submarine warfare without restriction. These two aspects of German policy—one relating to
land and the other to sea power—were
not inherently antagonistic. The reservations entertained in 1916 by Bethmann-
Hollweg and his civilian colleagues were
based on the feeling that to challenge

British maritime supremacy attempted
too much, placing Germany in danger of
losing all.

The factors determining American
policy in relation to the submarine are
not so clear. Obscurity arose in part from
the fact that the law of neutrality, subject to the pressures of total war, was
incapable of reconciling neutral and belligerent interests, and the fiasco in 1914–
17 of the traditional rules of maritime
warfare explains in some measure at
least why the United States arrived at
an impasse with Germany. But pressure
upon American rights came from the
British as well as the German side.
During the two and one-half years pre-

---

ceding the rupture in German-American relations, Great Britain had imposed an ever-tightening control over the flow of neutral commerce. As early as March 1915, a British Order in Council not only placed trade to and from Germany under penalty of confiscation, but subjected to close supervision the trade of the outside world with neutrals bordering on Germany. The American Government protested that the measure was "a practical assertion of unlimited belligerent rights over neutral commerce within the whole European area, and an almost unqualified denial of the sovereign rights of the nations now at peace." Why, notwithstanding, did ominous crises in Anglo-American relations fail to develop? Or considering that both Great Britain and Germany waged war on the basis of military necessity in disregard of the rules of maritime warfare, why did not the United States retreat before a world at war? This latter query is particulary pertinent because such a withdrawal was precisely the object of the so-called neutrality legislation enacted from 1935 to 1939.

During the first World War the American bias in favor of Great Britain and against Germany was from the outset very great. The reasons for this bias were several—some of them, as we have seen, going back into the nineteenth century, a period in which American-British relations were cast in a mold of accommodation. With the beginning of the World War the Germans further prejudiced their case by use of the submarine. And meanwhile, American fortunes were being ever more strongly tied to Great Britain by a rapidly developing wartime trade. This trade quickly swelled to such proportions that American domestic prosperity virtually depended upon it.

It was perhaps only to be expected, therefore, that a popular postwar explanation of American involvement in the first World War, an explanation most widely accepted during the 1930's, was that American policy toward Europe in 1914–17—friendship toward Britain, enmity toward Germany—was a direct result of the economic situation.

I

At the simplest level, publicists in the 1930's ascribed American participation in the first World War to the influence of munitions makers. Investigations in the United States and elsewhere, together with numerous books and articles, revealed questionable practices of munitions makers in conducting their business. Much evidence was adduced that these manufacturers artificially stimulated markets abroad, and within their respective countries urged armament expenditures and a belligerent foreign policy. It was an unsavory picture which lent itself to exaggerated conclusions about self-seeking munitions makers as a cause of war.

But this argument is inapplicable to American participation in the first World War. As Wilson's secretary of war, Newton D. Baker, wrote during the thirties, it was "easy to demonstrate that the condition of cotton farmers . . . was infintely more a subject of concern and anxiety on the part of the Government . . . than the interest or welfare of the munitions makers." In 1914, moreover, "there was no munitions industry in the United States . . . and by 1917 the industry in that field which had been created here, either by or on behalf of the Allied nations, was merely a part of America's industrial plant diverted from peacetime to wartime production."

The charge against munitions makers was "a singular selection of a particular group out of a much larger and quite indiscriminate mass."

Rather than searching for direct influence by munitions makers on the government, it is more germane to ask whether the volume of munitions shipped by the United States to the Allies played an important role in prompting Germany to decide for unrestricted submarine warfare.

The wartime trade of the United States with England, France, Italy, Russia, and Canada represented an increase of 184 per cent, from a total of $3,445,-000,000 for the period 1911–13 (these are fiscal years ending June 30) to $9,-796,000,000 for the comparable three-year period 1915–17. Difficulty of definition makes it hard to determine the proportion of this latter amount represented by munitions. From June 30, 1914, to June 30, 1917, the United States shipped $506,674,000 worth of gunpowder and $665,237,000 in other explosives. Firearms were sent in the amount of $113,-229,000; cartridges, $104,022,000; and barbed wire, $45,104,000. Metals, in various states of semi-manufacture, were shipped: zinc, $98,302,000; steel, $182,-577,000; brass, $553,625,000; and copper, $551,779,000. In all these instances (except copper, where the increase was 277 per cent) the increase over the three-year period 1911–13 was so extreme as to indicate that before the war the countries in question imported these commodities from the United States in only negligible quantities.

The sum representing "essential war materials" which was arrived at in connection with the Senate investigation of the munitions industry was $2,167,-000,000, which would be 23 per cent of the United States's trade with the designated countries. The remainder of the trade was only indirectly related to actual battle, but it was no less important to the Allied war economy. Wheat was shipped in the amount of $581,509,000, an increase of 683 per cent; wheat flour, $112,068,000, a 205 per cent increase; sugar, $130,533,000, 3,883 per cent; and meat, $469,863,867, 240 per cent.

There was indeed bitter resentment in Germany over the shipment of munitions by the United States to the Allies, evidence of which occurred again and again in the dispatches of the American ambassador. In April 1915 Germany formally protested such shipments, alleging that "an entirely new industry" which had hardly existed in the United States before the war was being created, and that despite the theoretical willingness of this industry to supply Germany it was "actually delivering goods only to the enemies of Germany." Nonetheless our examination . . . of Germany's decision for unrestricted submarine warfare does not suggest that this very natural resentment was the controlling factor in Germany's action; in fact, an absence of munitions in the American trade with the Allies could hardly have altered the chain of circumstances leading to the impasse over the submarine. We have seen that the British wheat supply and the tonnage available to the British trade were primary objects of German attack. Germany was striking at the whole British economy and aiming at total victory, just as Britain through the blockade was striking at the whole German economy and was likewise unreceptive to a negotiated peace. American trade was of the utmost usefulness to the Allies, but its significance did not turn solely on munitions; it attached just as much to the nonmilitary content of the trade.

Actually the portion of the hearings which the so-called Nye Committee, the Special Congressional Committee Investigating the Munitions Industry, devoted to American entrance into the war did not, despite the committee's appellation, pin the blame on munitions makers so much as upon bankers. Indeed, the importance of finance in ensuring in 1914–17 the flow of American goods to the Allies cannot be questioned, and this aspect of America's relation to the war calls for a close examination.

The bulk of American shipments was paid for by the Allies through the sizable balance which the United States owed Great Britain on the outbreak of the war; through wartime export of goods, services, and gold to the United States; and through sale of securities in the American financial market. By the time the United States entered the war, however, the British, French, Russian, and Italian Governments owed private American investors $2,260,827,000. Leaving out of account Canadian purchases, which to April 1917 had required for war purposes only $120,000,000 in credit, this means that 27 per cent of the American exports to the Allied countries was financed by publicly issued bonds and other forms of credit in the United States.

Reliance by the belligerents on American money was a prospect which the Wilson Administration had frowned upon at the beginning of the war. When in August 1914 J. P. Morgan and Company had inquired whether the State Department would object to the making of private loans to belligerents, the reply had been that such loans would be "inconsistent with the true spirit of neutral-

ity." Before stating this position Bryan had presented the problem to Wilson, arguing that "money is the worst form of all contrabands because it commands everything else," that expressions of sympathy for one side or the other would be intensified "if each group was pecuniarily interested in the success of the nation to whom its members had loaned money," and that the "powerful financial interests . . . would be tempted to use their influence through the newspapers to support the interests of the government to which they had loaned because the value of the security would be affected by the result of the war." Yet at this stage Bryan's concluding observation was alone decisive: "The floating of these loans would absorb the loanable funds and might affect our ability to borrow."

The Government's objection to loans was not based on statutory authority. Nevertheless the eventual abandonment of the policy did not result from its extra-legal character. To be viable, such a financial restriction required a willingness by the various elements in the American economy to accept a falling off of export business. Ultimately the restriction succumbed to an irresistible combination of forces: commercial need and American sympathy for the Allied cause.

The financial ban was modified as early as October 1914 when the State Department made a distinction between loans and short-term credits, thus permitting an extension of $10,000,000 in credit to the French Government by the National City Bank of New York. By mid-1915 an additional $100,000,000 of private funds had been made available in one form or another to the French and Russian Governments. The question of a large public loan, which could not be indefinitely avoided, became acute in August 1915 when sterling exchange, which until then had been pegged by purchases of J. P. Morgan and Company, began to decline in value. If dollars could not be borrowed, Great Britain would have to ship gold in large quantities, a hazardous operation in wartime. A wholesale transfer of the metal would also have had undesirable monetary repercussions both in England and the United States. Another alternative, but one which the British Government was understandably reluctant to adopt, was the large-scale liquidation of British-owned securities.

Writing to Wilson in August 1915, Secretary of the Treasury William G. McAdoo said that it was "imperative for England to establish a large credit in this country." In his opinion the position taken in August 1914 was "most illogical and inconsistent. We approve and encourage sales of supplies to England and others but we disapprove the creation by them of credit balances here to finance their lawful and welcome purchases. . . . To maintain our prosperity we must finance it. Otherwise it may stop and that would be disastrous." Contrasting the nation's credit resources with those of a year earlier, he said that they were "simply marvellous now. They are easily 5 to 6 billion dollars." Lansing wrote to the President in similar vein on September 6. Pointing out that American exports in 1915 would exceed imports by an estimated two and a half billion dollars, he said that the European countries must find the dollars to pay for this excess of purchases or "they will have to stop buying and our present export trade will shrink proportionately. The result would be restriction of output, industrial depression, idle capital and idle labor, numerous failures, financial demoralization, and general unrest and suffering among the laboring classes." Observing that "we have more money than we can use," Lansing felt that "the practical reasons for discouraging loans have largely disappeared." Moreover, he believed that "popular sympathy has become crystallized in favor of one or another of the belligerents to such an extent that the purchase of bonds would in no way increase the bitterness of partisanship." The upshot was that the earlier policy was now discarded. In October 1915 a joint Anglo-French loan of $500,000,000 was floated.

Recognizing that general commercial considerations rather than the narrow financial interests of bankers forced the change in Administration policy, one must still ask whether the loans, having been made, created a stake in Allied victory which then proceeded to determine governmental policy. That such a connection existed was widely believed by popular and congressional opinion in the thirties. A typical assertion was that of Senator Gerald Nye himself that "When Americans went into the fray they little thought that they were . . . fighting to save the skins of American bankers who had bet too boldly on the outcome of the war and had two billions of dollars of loans to the Allies in jeopardy."

This assumption is actually more revealing of the postwar intellectual climate than it is of the factors leading to American entrance into war in 1917. Sympathy for the Allied cause among leading New York bankers—such as J. P. Morgan, who had long operated London and Paris offices—greatly facilitated the financial accommodation of the Allies. Rather than following as a consequence, partisanship preceded the making of the loans. Still more to the point is the fact that the diplomatic record, which made it virtually impossible for the United States to pull back in 1917, had already been substantially completed in the autumn of 1915; by that time the Wilson Administration had set its course on the question of neutral rights. The final crystallization of the American policy of neutrality in the first four months of 1916 cannot reasonably be attributed to anxiety over the safety of Allied loans, which had begun to be sizable only in the autumn of 1915.

It is also necessary to point out that the greater part of the Allied indebtedness at the time of American entry into the war was secured with American, other neutral, and British imperial (chiefly Canadian) collateral. In the instance of the three United Kingdom loans totaling $800,000,000 (negotiated between September 1916 and February 1917), the value of the collateral, duly advertised to the investing public, actually amounted to 120 per cent of the face value of the bonds. Unsecured indebtedness at the time of the American declaration of war stood at $855,000,000. The Anglo-French loan of October 1915, which was publicly issued, accounted for $500,000,000 of this total; and the remainder was mainly in the form of acceptances and other bank credits. Even as regards the unsecured obligations of the Allied Governments, the hypothesis that the bankers and their clients were anxious over their investments has not been supported with evidence. An important negative test of the prevailing attitude in the United States is the absence of any movement to escape loss by selling Allied bonds in the market. Finally, there has been only supposition, without actual demonstration, that Administration officials and congressmen

felt themselves under pressure to assure the collectibility of the loans.

II

Rejecting these explanations of American involvement which blame the cupidity or anxiety of particular interest groups, such as the bankers or munitions makers, we still must examine the proposition, which is implied generally in the economic interpretation, that the response of the American economy as a whole to the golden opportunity for trade with the Allies was the basic factor in the break with Germany.

It is obvious that the swollen trade with the Allies, representing vitally important aid purchased with cash and loans, far exceeded the normal export requirements of the American economy. The resulting prosperity was pleasing to the American Government, but the direction, content, and volume of the trade was not the result of any positive policy adopted in Washington. For all the record shows, the Administration was merely acquiescing in the operations of the free market and the profit motive. Indeed, the economic argument is essentially that a shortsighted yielding to the promptings of commercial gain resulted in the United States becoming a base of supplies for the Allies, thus compromising German-American relations. By permitting the decisions of the market place to prevail, the American Government, it is contended, allowed the nation to drift into dangerous waters.

This argument can be made still more precise. Germany was dissatisfied not only because of the large trade which the Allies enjoyed with the United States, but also because American neutrality had for Germany herself no economic value. German-American trade declined to an insignificant trickle, removing any possibility of an economic deterrent to unleashing the submarine. Trade with the Allies, the argument runs, took on such large and profitable proportions that the American defense of neutral rights against the arbitrary encroachments of the Allies became progressively weaker. Moreover, after the economy had become abnormally dependent on Allied markets, any attempt to correct the imbalance became impractical. Economic retaliation against England's flagrant violation of the rules of blockade, search and seizure, and contraband would not have been feasible; such measures would have had serious repercussions, stemming not alone from the American action, but also from retaliatory acts which Great Britain was in a position to apply with great effect.

In September 1916 when resentment against the British black list of German-influenced firms and against British censorship of mail was at a high pitch, Congress at the Administration's request passed legislation giving the President discretionary power to discriminate in specified ways against belligerents who were interfering with American commerce. Exploring the practicality of employing the authorized measures, the State Department requested an opinion from the Commerce Department on what could be done "that would be effective and, at the same time, least injurious to this country." The latter department, on the basis of a closely reasoned analysis, concluded that "reprisals . . . afford no assurance of success, and threaten even the present basis of neutral commerce." It was pointed out in the supporting argument that in the

belligerent countries, war for the moment is supreme; commercial considerations take a subordinate place. We can attack their commerce but our own commerce will unavoid-

ably suffer in consequence even more than it has suffered from the restriction placed on it by the countries at war. There is little likelihood by these means of obtaining the withdrawal of the objectionable regulations. Counterreprisals would be almost inevitable. . . . At present, rubber, wool, jute, tin, plumbago, and certain other raw products essential to our industries are under export prohibition in Great Britain and in the various colonies and self-governing dominions which are the principal source of supply. Shipments of these articles have been continuously imported into the United States from British countries, however, under special agreements between the British Government and associations of leading importers of the various products. It is obvious that by a termination of these agreements, Great Britain could paralyze many of our industries.

The memorandum stated that an embargo on munitions would be the most effective measure, but that compared with the earlier period its impact would be dulled because additional factories in Britain had since been converted into munitions plants. Indeed, an embargo "might, in practice, effect the cancellation of a contract more highly regarded by the American concern than by the British Government."

In short, the American Government permitted the Allies to monopolize the American market as a base of supplies. This monopoly not only invited German attack but made it difficult for the United States, whose prosperity had become in part dependent on a continuance of the Allied trade, to forestall it. This is the strongest form in which the economic argument can be put. It errs in viewing the clash between the United States and Germany as a result solely of the complications of wartime trade, but it has the merit of stating the case without resort to scapegoats. Indeed, it permits recognition of the fact that more than a purely private interest was involved in America's trade with warring Europe. A great war must inevitably affect the economy of neutral nations. The doctrine of freedom of the seas, therefore, cannot be dismissed as synonymous with the freedom of "hucksters" to make money. It is related to a real national interest which a government can sacrifice but not deny. It presents a problem, moreover, which is not eliminated by the mere fact of substituting governmental authority for the private decisions of the market place.

When the hard realities of the economic problem with which the United States was confronted in the first World War are considered, the so-called neutrality legislation of the 1930's, which denied to American citizens the traditional benefits of freedom of the seas, seems unrealistic. Yet if the legislation was unduly stringent in limiting the economic transactions and freedom of movement of American citizens in time of war, it erred on the right rather than the wrong side. It precluded any danger in the second World War of American policy being shaped, whether in reality or merely in appearance, by considerations of trade and travel incidental to the war itself. Based on the supposition that trade was the dominant strand in our relations with Europe, the legislation, however, failed to measure up to the requirements of the time. Actually the United States could not insulate itself from European turmoil merely by foregoing commercial relations with belligerents. Within a month after outbreak of the second World War the embargo on sale of munitions to belligerents was repealed. Subsequently the ban on arming American merchantmen was lifted. Then the neutrality legislation was completely by-passed by adoption of Lend-Lease in

March 1941 and the special naval measures taken that summer and autumn to protect shipments to Britain. None of these important moves by the Roosevelt Administration was made for commercial reasons.

American policy in the interwar years responded not to current events as they unfolded but to certain theories explaining our involvement in the first World War. Of course, the fact that the legislation of the thirties failed to accomplish its purpose does not argue against the interpretation of the past on which it was based. It may be assumed, however, that the first experience was sufficiently similar to the second to have constituted fair warning, and that our own perverse misreading of the past assisted fate in preparing a repetition of the ordeal.

It has been shown that wartime trade confronted the Wilson Administration with the necessity of making various legal and economic decisions. But a political decision, however disguised, was also required, for the problem of trade was basically more political than it was legal or economic. Germany was vastly disturbed that neutral trade went not to the Central Powers but to Great Britain and the other Allies. The various neutral governments by legal and economic measures could modify the one-sided trade situation in its superficial aspects, but they could accomplish no fundamental change without making a political decision involving their relations with Britain. British control of the seas and of the products of a vast non-European area, colonial and otherwise—a control which had been exercised for decades and even centuries—was at the bottom of Germany's quarrel with Great Britain. Nothing short of virtual reversal of the existing trade situation, which would have denied trade to the Allies and made it available to Germany, would have been considered by her military and naval officials as an acceptable reason for curbing the submarine. It was their highest objective to achieve a disposition of sea power for the future which would assure precisely this result, toward which German naval policy since the turn of the century had in fact been directed.

If, by breaching the British blockade, the United States could have achieved a major shift in the direction of neutral trade, Germany would undoubtedly have abstained from ruthless assault on world shipping, for she would then have accomplished her end through virtual alliance with the United States. But, unlike Germany, the United States was not rebellious against Britain's predominant position. The argument that this showed subservience to Great Britain, so long as American prosperity was not endangered, does not cover the whole ground. It sprang mainly from the fact that the United States saw no threat to its vital interests in Britain's position and, moreover, shrank from the prospect of Germany supplanting British power. This essential difference between American and German attitudes toward Great Britain underlay the progressive estrangement and eventual rupture of German-American relations.

In an effort to adjust itself to the European war, the United States at first sought refuge behind the traditional rules of maritime warfare. But these rules, at best heavily weighted in favor of already established sea power and sorely beset by technological innovations, provided poor protection from Germany's constant probings. Thus the United States was in an exposed position, highly vulnerable to German pressure even had the American attitude toward Germany been without bias. In the actual event the pro-Allied character of American policy lent to German actions, already based on military necessity, a certain moral justification which still further facilitated German disregard for the rules.

The bias in American policy was obscured for the United States—but not for Germany—by the fact that the economic and political aspects of American policy overlapped. The situation in 1914–17 was such that the demand for wartime trade could be indulged without running counter to the Administration's underlying judgment regarding the ultimate political consequences of the war's outcome. Thus economic and political factors reinforced each other and, even in retrospect, defy separation. This particular combination of factors was, however, purely fortuitous. If because of well-established commercial contacts and the existing disposition of sea power, our trade relations had been facilitated with the side not in political favor—as subsequently happened in the case of the Sino-Japanese war in 1937 and after—the American Government would have had to separate the strands of its policy. This would have been extremely difficult in 1914–17 for there was no basic agreement of American public opinion on what the national interest required.

Had the German Government confined its use of the submarine to unannounced attack on armed enemy merchantmen, as Bethmann-Hollweg had urged, the economic and political aspects of American policy would have been forced apart, clarifying perhaps the basis on which the American Government was acting. But Germany was so intent on overwhelming the British that she failed to exploit the confusion in American policy.

A notable attempt to treat domestic and diplomatic history as parts of one whole rather than as separate subjects is ERNEST R. MAY's *The World War and American Isolation, 1914–1917* (1959). May's conclusion, more fatalistic than determinist, that the period 1914–1917 could hardly have ended other than it did differs sharply from both the Seymour and Barnes interpretations, but the role he assigns in the selection below to German domestic pressures in the submarine decision of 1917 does lend support to Seymour. The allure of the submarine weapon to most Germans may be better understood by recalling how many Americans, frustrated by the indecisiveness of the Korean conflict, clamored for the use of another weapon—the atomic bomb—that promised quick victory.*

German Domestic Pressures and the Submarine

Far more important than the rebuff to Wilson's mediation hopes was the German decision to open a submarine campaign against merchant shipping. Other acts might have aroused moral disapproval by the United States, but little else could have generated a genuine antagonism. There were no American interests within reach of German land forces. The one method by which Germany could stir the United States to threaten war was by ordering submarines to attack neutral ships and belligerent passenger carriers. Yet the German government chose to issue such an order.

Unlike the decision to reject mediation, this action was only partly a product of necessity. It came about almost accidentally. Submarines achieved surprise successes at a time when no other German forces were making news. Certain naval officers elected to champion wider use of the weapon, deliberately stirring public hopes. Since other officials failed to look deeply enough into the implications of these proposals, the publicity was allowed to run unchecked. As a result of its success, coupled with the relative absence of reflective opposition, a decision in favor of a submarine campaign was taken almost in a fit of absence of mind.

The process that led to this decision commenced in September, 1914. Early in the month a submarine chanced upon

* Reprinted by permission of the publishers from Ernest R. May, *The World War and American Isolation, 1914–1917*, Cambridge, Mass.: Harvard University Press. Copyright 1959, by the President and Fellows of Harvard College. Pp. 113–122, 197–205.

the British cruiser *Pathfinder* and sank her. In the latter part of the month, a combination of bad weather and administrative inefficiency in the British Admiralty threw three more cruisers into the path of a U-boat. The aged vessels *Cressy, Hogue,* and *Aboukir Bay* were torpedoed off the Broad Fourteens by the small, slow U-9, a gasoline-burning submarine already considered obsolete.

One consequence of these accidental successes was an arousal in the navy of enthusiasm for wider use of U-boats. Theretofore the vessels had been regarded as experimental and, at most, as auxiliary arms of the fleet. Hardly anyone had conceived of the U-boat as an independent weapon operating against enemy commerce. After the September exploits, this novel idea began to spread through the fleet. Tirpitz and various officers in the Navy Ministry became interested. By early November the Chief of the Naval Staff had decided to urge such a course upon the Chancellor and the Emperor. By the turn of the year nearly all the higher ranks of the navy had become engaged in energetic agitation for a U-boat campaign.

It is easy to understand this emergent enthusiasm. The navy had been useless in the early stages of the war. The High Seas Fleet had stood inactive while Britain cleared the oceans and established her dominance over the North Sea. While the army struggled to preserve and increase the Fatherland, the navy remained merely decorative, and its officers felt wounded not only in pride but also in hope. "If we come to the end . . . without the fleet having bled and worked," wrote Tirpitz, "we shall get nothing more for the fleet, and all the scanty money that there may be will be spent on the army. The great efforts of His Majesty the Emperor to make Germany a naval power will have been all in vain." The September triumphs awakened hopes that the navy might be able, after all, to help win the war.

How these natural feelings overcame the judgment of so many officers is somewhat harder to understand. The U-boats available for operations in the North Sea area were but twenty-one in number. Twelve of these were slow, gasoline-powered, and capable of operating only in the Channel region. Only nine were diesel craft that could reach England's western coasts, and the largest carried but ten torpedoes. In view of the quantity of British shipping, it required considerable imagination to envision a successful blockade. The only prewar estimate, indeed, called for a force of two hundred and twenty-one submarines equipped with devices not yet designed. Some officers remained aware of the discrepancy between the idea and the means available to execute it.

But the majority submerged their doubts. Neutral shipowners, they reasoned, would be frightened away from English ports. If the campaign were masked as retaliation against British interference with trade, neutral governments might even cooperate in the blockade. A few sinkings would meanwhile strike such terror into English shippers as to halt sailings. Many officers relied on a hypothetical account, printed before the war, of England's strangulation by a handful of submarines. This confidence-inspiring estimate had appeared in *The Strand* magazine over the name of Sir Arthur Conan Doyle. When an admiral was asked after the war to explain the Naval Staff's miscalculations he indicated blushingly that the navy had put too much faith in Sherlock Holmes.

From this irrational enthusiasm in the navy grew a public cry for the opening of a submarine campaign against British commerce. The idea was thrown dramatically into the public arena by Tirpitz. In an interview with an American journalist, Karl von Wiegand, the Grand Admiral declared, "England wants to starve us. We can play the same game. We can bottle her up and destroy every ship that endeavors to break the blockade." When asked if Germany had enough U-boats, he replied vehemently and misleadingly, "Yes, we are superior to England in submarines of the larger types." Published in late December, this interview attracted wide notice. The idea of striking England's vitals with the U-boat weapon had received the authoritative imprimatur of the navy's elder statesman.

The seed dropped by Tirpitz rooted in fallow ground. It is unlikely that the desperate frustration of the government was widely shared. Few knew the extent to which operations in the west had failed. Official reports had so disguised the importance of the Marne engagements that they had passed almost unnoticed. The clamor aroused by Tirpitz's interview was probably not spontaneous; the newspapers that most strongly supported his plan were those most closely identified with the Navy Ministry. But a feeling must have been growing that moated England was responsible for the war's prolongation. There was thus a favorable atmosphere for a secret weapon delusion.

The Grand Admiral's proposal soon found support among party leaders. It appealed to the Anglophobia of the right. Offering also a promise of swift triumph, it fitted in with annexationist dreams. When the government seemed to delay adopting the proposal, vexation developed. Even Erzberger, the left Centrist, published a pamphlet, *No Sentimentality*, calling for immediate institution of a ruthless submarine blockade. When Bethmann visited Berlin, he found deputies accusing him of pro-British leanings. And not even the left socialists opposed this clamor. By the spring of 1915, there seemed to have risen a U-boat fervor comparable to the annexationist passion.

The government was not so powerless before this movement as it was before the annexationist fever. The Foreign Ministry had an opportunity to kill the Tirpitz interview, which it blunderingly failed to seize. The text was sent to the Ministry for censorship. When the responsible officer, Count Mumm, read it through, he received the impression that Wiegand had already cabled it to America. It had, in fact, gone in a diplomatic pouch, and its publication could still have been stopped. But Mumm assumed that it would be printed overseas and therefore could not be kept from German editors. After telling Zimmermann about it, he authorized its release to the press.

Even after the interview's publication, there remained some chance of cooling public enthusiasm. The truth about Germany's limited capabilities could have been spread before party leaders as it was later. But Bethmann and his associates did not oppose the movement, partly from mistaken information, partly from irresolution, but largely from simple failure to foresee its consequences.

Chance played a part, too, in the ultimate approval of the blockade plan, but Bethmann was alerted by this time to the need for careful calculation. Every political aspect of the proposal was surveyed, at least superficially, in the Foreign Ministry and the Chancellery. On various grounds Bethmann postponed its adoption.

He was concerned, first of all, about possible effects on neutrals, especially those of southern Europe. Should a submarine campaign pit Germany against all neutrals, Italy and the entire Balkan peninsula might fall into the Allied camp. Since the army General Staff held that Germany could not stand such an addition to the number of her enemies, this possibility threw a dark shadow over the Chancellor's thoughts on U-boat warfare.

The United States was secondary in his thinking. Bernstorff and his aides had faithfully reported America's strong sympathy for the Allies. They had also made clear her dedication to profitable trade. From Wilson's legalistic pronouncements against interference with business, Bethmann might foresee an American outcry against a submarine decree, but he had little reason to fear war. "President Wilson said to me," wrote Bernstorff in his first personal report to Bethmann, " 'We must be absolutely neutral, because otherwise our mixed population would fall into another war.' " The ambassador stressed time and again America's consuming desire for peace, and he reported continual though slight improvement in America's attitude toward Germany, crediting the improvement to fear of Japan, to Britain's heavy-handed censorship, to the mine war zone decree, and to the achievements of German arms: " 'Nothing succeeds like success' is still a fundamental principle of Americans, and he who has success will always find friends." Receiving this report in late December, Bethmann read it carefully and underlined sections. It suggested that a successful blockade of Britain might turn American sympathies toward Germany. But the United States remained a question mark.

Rendering his preliminary verdict on the blockade plan, Bethmann gave more weight to uncertainty about the neutrals than to arguments advanced by the admirals. Shortly after receiving the first recommendation from Admiral Hugo von Pohl, the Chief of the Naval Staff, he asked the Foreign Ministry for an estimate of neutral reactions and received a further warning that the small neutrals, Italy, and the United States were all unpredictable. The submarine blockade should be instituted, he was advised, only if the military situation were so favorable as to make it folly for any neutral to take the Allied side. Answering Pohl, the Chancellor gave due regard to this advice. Though conceding the desirability of striking England with any and all weapons, he detailed the possible political consequences. Italy and Rumania might declare war, and all the European neutrals might halt exports to Germany. "Although America, because of its lack of military forces, can hardly declare war on us," the Chancellor stated, "still it is capable of proclaiming a trade boycott against us, like that of England, as well as pushing forward, to some extent officially, the export of war material to our enemies." American antipathy toward Japan would no longer hinder the Allies from bringing Japanese troops to Europe, and the United States might join the campaign to destroy German commerce. "The thoughts of the Foreign Office," Bethmann assured Pohl, "are not of a legalistic nature, but they result from considerations of military-political opportunity.

The question is not *if*, but *when* the measure may be taken without harm to our situation. . . . This moment seems today still not to have arrived."

Bethmann clung to these doubts throughout most of January. Arguing the question before the Kaiser on January 9 [1915], Bethmann presented his case "very aptly and calmly." Although Pohl contested each of the Chancellor's reservations, he failed to overcome them. The Kaiser ruled, "U-boat commerce war shall for the time being be postponed, until the present uncertainty of the political situation has cleared. Then shall the All-Highest be asked anew for a decision. In the meantime the U-boats are to be readied for commerce warfare." Bethmann was not fighting the admirals as he was to do later. He was simply holding them back until a propitious time.

Although the political air failed to clear, Bethmann's doubts began to yield. Italy and the Balkan governments grew steadily less friendly, and it came to seem as if restraint on Germany's part would not, in any case, hold them back from war. The United States meanwhile issued its protest against British interference with trade. Reports from Washington indicated a widening breach between the Allies and the United States. The pro-German Queen of Sweden urged the Kaiser to declare a U-boat blockade, and the Naval Staff passed on intelligence reports indicating passivity, if not enthusiasm, in Norway and the Netherlands.

Pressure on the Chancellor meanwhile grew fierce. It came, first of all, from the Naval Staff. Growing more and more insistent, Pohl proclaimed that the blockade had to come at once. England had only six or seven weeks of food supplies, he declared, but she would soon begin to receive Argentine grain. Once this grain was in her warehouses, England could hold out indefinitely against a blockade. Germany's own food stocks were meanwhile dwindling. The Interior Ministry had grossly overestimated the harvest, making it necessary for the government to ration food. Economists joined with the admirals, therefore, in urging a submarine blockade of Britain, just as Zimmermann and others of the Foreign Office ceased to advise against it. Impressed also with the enthusiasm of the public, Bethmann felt unable to resist any longer.

He capitulated quickly. After conferring with Tirpitz, he met with Pohl, Zimmermann, Falkenhayn, and Interior Minister Clemens von Delbrück. All insisted that the submarine blockade be imposed as soon as possible. Bethmann still worried whether Germany had enough U-boats for the purpose, but Pohl assured him categorically that the fleet was ready. The Chancellor felt concern about Belgium. If American relief shipments were halted, Germany would have to feed the Belgians from her own slender stocks. Delbrück eased his mind on this score, and Bethmann went home from this conference with most of his doubts suppressed. On the following day, February 2, his reservations broke entirely. After a conference with Zimmermann and the Treasury Minister, Karl Helfferich, he telephoned Pohl and told him to go ahead and submit to the Kaiser a decree declaring all the waters around Britain a submarine war zone.

Since Pohl was leaving the Naval Staff to take command of the High Seas Fleet, he moved quickly to secure the Kaiser's consent. He wanted the decree to be his last official act. The imminence of his departure from the Naval Staff had, in all probability, spurred him during the entire month. It certainly led him to evade routine in approaching the Emperor, for he did not clear the decree with Tirpitz as he should have. Nor did he permit the cautious Chief of the Naval Cabinet to hear of it. At Wilhelmshaven, where the Kaiser came on February 4 to install Pohl in his new command, the admiral cornered the Emperor in the bow of a motor launch. With Tirpitz, Müller, and the rest of the imperial entourage sitting in the after-part of the boat, unable to hear above the motor's roar, Pohl asked the Kaiser to approve a war zone decree. The Emperor nodded his consent. Pohl published a notice that day, over his own signature, and the Foreign Office sent a prearranged dispatch to the neutral capitals.

The waters around Great Britain and Ireland, declared the Navy and Foreign Ministries, were to become a war zone on February 18. Germany "will endeavor to destroy every enemy merchant ship that is found in this area of war," the dispatch warned, "without its always being possible to avert the peril, that thus threatens persons and cargoes. Neutrals are therefore warned against further entrusting crews, passengers and wares to such ships." Since English vessels sometimes hid under neutral flags, the warning went on, neutral ships ought not to enter the war zone. "[T]heir becoming victims of torpedoes directed against enemy ships cannot always be avoided. . . . The German Government . . . ," the dispatch concluded, "may expect that the neutral powers will show no less consideration for the vital interests of Germany than for those of England and will aid in keeping their citizens and the property of the latter

from this area. This is the more to be expected, as it must be in the interest of the neutral powers to see this destructive war end as soon as possible."

The decree of February 4 had been issued without full consideration of possible American reactions. When Wilson denounced it, the government suddenly realized the danger of drawing America into the war. Although the admirals expressed willingness to run this risk, Bethmann disagreed, holding American intervention to be a calamity which Germany should industriously avoid, and there commenced the running battle that was to continue for two years. . . .

* * *

After the spring of 1915, the burden of choice between war and peace lay upon the German government. Wilson had apparently threatened war if U-boats were allowed to attack passenger liners. By declaring that his demands on Germany were quite independent of any made upon Britain, he encouraged no hope that the threat might be lifted. Germany had to deny herself the use of the weapon in order to keep the peace or else strike at England and risk war. Chancellor Bethmann Hollweg had no doubt that the more important aim was to keep America neutral, and he was prepared to sacrifice the U-boat campaign or any part of it in order to keep the peace. Neither the Navy Ministry nor the Naval Staff agreed with him; the admirals insisted that the submarine weapon should be used to the full, come what might, and their pleas were supported by powerful blocs among the Reichstag and the public. It was necessarily Germany's policy, therefore, to carry on the U-boat war at whatever pitch the United States would allow. The result, both internationally and internally, was a rising rhythm of lull and crisis.

To temporize was, of course, Bethmann's way. He was scarcely a figure of fire and granite. But circumstances made it literally impossible for him to choose one of the drastic alternatives. He could not decide to abandon the submarine permanently. The Kaiser probably could not have been brought to approve such a policy, and, in any case, the decision would have shaken the unity of the nation, cut the Chancellor off from the Reichstag and the country, and perhaps imperiled the foundations of the Empire. Nor, on the other hand, could Bethmann bring himself to opt for an unrestricted U-boat campaign. Neither his conscience nor his political judgment would allow him to do so.

He was convinced that the submarine could not achieve decisive results in the war with England. "A peace forced upon England by the U-boat war," he wrote, "would be equivalent to public acknowledgment that England's supremacy at sea had been destroyed by Germany's sea power. Before England would make up her mind to make such an acknowledgment, she would sacrifice the last man and the last penny." The best impartial advice given him was to the effect that, in the first place, the submarines could stop only a fraction of Britain's imports and, in the second place, that ruthlessness on Germany's part merely intensified the English will to fight.

He was also certain that an all-out U-boat campaign would bring the United States into the war, with disastrous results for Germany. "It is absolutely beyond doubt," he said to the Reichstag budget committee, "that if today I proclaim a ruthless U-boat war, tomorrow America will have broken with us." The effect of such a break, he believed, would be to bring all the European neutrals into the war on the Allied side. The newspapers of the Netherlands, the Scandinavian states, and even Switzerland, indicated that their governments would follow America's lead. Bethmann predicted that the Dutch would enter the war as soon as Germany and the United States broke relations; the Allies not only would obtain reinforcement from Holland's small but well-trained army but, even more important, would gain access by sea to the rear of the German lines. Among the crucial Balkan states, too, he found the American question almost decisive. "The attitude of the United States toward us," he declared during the *Arabic* crisis, "causes every other possible state to stiffen against us; it is, for example, an unmistakable barometer for the attitude of the Balkan states."

Quite apart from its effect on European neutrals, the intervention of the United States would in itself, Bethmann thought, have cataclysmic results for Germany. There is a memorandum in the Secret File of the Foreign Ministry Archives which, if not Bethmann's, at least reflects his views. Itemizing the probable results of armed intervention by the United States, it mentions the financing of Germany's enemies, a doubling of their munitions imports, a reinforcement of Allied armies by the enlistment of American volunteers, "liquidation of the Balkans," and privations for Germany herself. Intervention by the United States, the Chancellor did assert, would prolong the war by two years, and unlimited U-boat war was therefore the *ultima ratio.* "It represents such a challenge," he declared in 1916, "that it [could] . . . signify *finis Germaniae.*"

Holding such views, Bethmann could not bring himself to sanction a defiant submarine campaign. Although he was temperamentally disinclined to battle for convictions, he could not allow the admirals to ignore political considerations, to bet on their optimistic estimates of the U-boat's capabilities, and to make war on the United States. He felt obliged to fight with every resource against a decision in favor of an unlimited U-boat campaign.

At the same time, he was almost incapable of forcing a decision to abandon the weapon. The admirals would not accept his reasoning. Tirpitz and the successive Chiefs of the Naval Staff staked their experience and professional reputations upon the prediction that an all-out campaign would bring England to her knees before American intervention could affect the outcome of the war. Bethmann could caution the admirals of dangers, but he could not change their minds. He was continually in the position of seeming to place political ahead of military considerations.

As one result, he depended very heavily on the support of the army, although the army did not accept all his premises. Falkenhayn thought the navy's proposals untimely rather than pernicious. Eager to believe the admirals' prophecies, he said repeatedly that submarine commanders should be given their freedom as soon as the military situation permitted. The general did not share Bethmann's dread of the United States herself. He feared only the Dutch and the Balkan states, who might break his western line or cut the link with Constan-

tinople. Falkenhayn would vote for postponement of an all-out U-boat campaign but not for abandonment. Had the Chancellor sought a drastic decision, the army would probably have joined the navy in opposing him.

Outside imperial councils, moreover, a decision to give up the U-boat would have met opposition in the Reichstag and among the public. The right-wing parties were fanatical in their enthusiasm for unrestricted U-boat war. Not only did they disagree with the Chancellor's reasoning, but they chafed at his temporizing policy and criticized it as openly as the *Burgfrieden* and the German political tradition permitted. In this attitude they were supported by a large segment of the *Zentrum* and even by Progressives.

The right-wing press challenged all the Chancellor's premises. It insisted, in the first place, that the U-boat could bring England to her knees. When a retired admiral published an article declaring that the submarine could not win the war, the journals that deigned to notice it commented with derision. The Hamburg Chamber of Commerce passed a resolution of condemnation, and two of the city's newspapers, the *Nachrichten* and the *Fremdenblatt,* denounced such writing as treasonable. When Captain Persius, the respected naval expert of the *Berliner Tageblatt,* suggested that the claims of U-boat enthusiasts might be exaggerated, even this modest warning provoked scorn and anger. Conservatives, Free Conservatives, National Liberals, and right Centrists would hear no denial of the U-boat's effectiveness.

They insisted, too, that no serious consequences were to be feared from war with the United States. At the time of the strict accountability note the *Ber-*

liner Zeitung declared of America, "She has no army, and her fleet would not dare to approach nearer our shores than does the English. The expulsion of Germans from America would mean her ruin. America's threats are simply ridiculous, and it is more than ridiculous to take them in earnest." The Conservative *Tägliche Rundschau* declared that Germany had nothing to lose except the nice new ships sitting idle in American harbors, and a writer in *Der Tag* pointed out contemptuously that the United States had shown herself too feeble even to deal with Mexico.

Nor was such comment confined to journals of the far right. The *Kölnische Volkszeitung*, a Centrist organ, declared that Americans would not go to war because they lacked the martial virtues, and war "requires so many sacrifices and destroys business." The Progressive *Vossische Zeitung* printed an article by the eminent classical scholar, Eduard Meyer, asserting that Wilson would not be able to go to war if he wanted to. Even the Social Democratic *Vorwärts*, which commented skeptically on Meyer's prediction, suggested that American pacifism was probably powerful enough to prevent armed retaliation against a German U-boat campaign. And challenges to this complacency were usually either mild, like the *Münchener Neueste Nachrichten*'s observation that Germany should keep the peace in order to protect German-Americans, or else bore the marks of official inspiration. Anton Meyer-Gerhardt, who had been one of Bethmann's agents in the United States, advertised the dangers of war, and the semiofficial *Kölnische Zeitung* warned against complacency. Although it would not be true to suggest that the public, as a whole, was nonchalant about America, it is the case that very few people outside the

government appeared to share the anxieties of the Chancellor.

The right-wing press claimed, as a result, to speak for the mass of German opinion. Ernst Reventlow of the *Deutsche Tageszeitung* asserted during the *Lusitania* crisis:

It is not too much to say that a profound and widespread excitement has seized the German people at the very suggestion that the German Empire can be expected to abandon the submarine war or to let it become an empty form. . . . We have innumerable proofs of the existence of this deep excitement in Germany. . . . Rarely has a measure of war been greeted with greater satisfaction and watched with more lively sympathy than the submarine war against Great Britain's commerce.

Count Westarp asserted that the leaders of all parties except the Social Democrats were united in opposition to any limitation of the submarine war, and Centrist and Progressive leaders went to the Chancellery with Conservatives and National Liberals to express support for the admirals. The dissent of the Social Democrats was relatively mild. Reprinting a declaration somewhat like Reventlow's, *Vorwärts* commented, "A large number of people are, as is well known, of quite another opinion." Even among Social Democrats, the U-boat fever had made inroads. When Scheidemann spoke in the Reichstag, defending concessions to the United States, he began by saying:

Gentlemen, the enemy powers rest their hopes on our economic exhaustion. England's effort is, with all means, to carry out the starvation war against our people. Against this attempt to strangle us, which is prosecuted without regard to international law and the rights of neutrals, a sharp defense is called for ("Very true!"—from the right). Here we fight for our existence ("Very true!" —from the left). We have the right on our side if we reply to the English hunger blockade with the U-boat war ("Very true!"—from the Social Democrats). No one can complain of that ("Very true!"—from the right).

Bethmann, in any case, accepted the Conservative estimate. "Our public opinion is 'whipped up,'" he complained to navy leaders. "It is absolutely criminal how . . . [the people] have behaved in this matter."

Confronted with such a state of parliamentary and public opinion, Bethmann could not easily carry a proposal to abandon the submarine weapon. He felt obliged, indeed, to make a public pretense of sympathy with the U-boat enthusiasts. At the outset of the *Lusitania* crisis, the official *Norddeutsche Allgemeine Zeitung* promised, "Every means that art and nature offer to overpower the enemy we shall inexorably and remorselessly employ." The Chancellor's collaborator, Foreign Minister Jagow, asserted before the budget committee of the Reichstag in August, 1915, that restriction of the U-boat campaign could never be considered by the government. And Bethmann himself assured the Conservative leaders, "what is necessary will, without any hesitation, be done."

The Chancellor could only attempt to moderate the public agitation. The press censors watched for articles directly critical of the government's policy, and several numbers of the Conservative *Kreuzzeitung* and *Deutsche Tageszeitung* were suppressed as a result. In official, semiofficial, and friendly newspapers, meanwhile, the government's policy was supported and justified. Defending censorship of the *Deutsche Tageszeitung*, the official *Norddeutsche Allgemeine Zeitung* declared:

In the first place the impression was given that official circles, simply for the sake of peace with America, contemplated abandoning the great power of the U-boat weapon, and, in the second place, the absurd statement was unhesitatingly made that the accession of America to the ranks of our enemies would be a matter of no consequence. . . . Those who bear the responsibility and who must balance danger against advantage are immune to taunts of timidity, feebleness, or cowardice. . . . But for the dignity of the nation and in the interests of foreign policy, this propaganda must be brought to an end.

The semiofficial *Kölnische Zeitung* introduced the public to the arguments that had been found effective with the General Staff, asserting during the *Arabic* crisis, for instance, "It must be emphasized once more that our most pressing problem is a free road to Constantinople, and we cannot get there if we burden ourselves with a new enemy." Similar words appeared in newspapers whose editors or correspondents were intimate with officials of the Foreign Ministry. The *Berliner Tageblatt*, the Berlin *Lokal-Anzeiger*, and the *Frankfurter Zeitung* aided in the effort to abate public excitement.

In order to prevent an unrestricted U-boat campaign, however, the Chancellor had to rely primarily upon maneuver and intrigue within the government. He could do no more than appease the public and the Reichstag. He could not appeal to them if a decision went against him in one of the Kaiser's councils. His antagonists, on the other hand, could always be consoled in defeat by the conviction that public opinion would ultimately bring them victory. Although circumstances gave to Germany the decision between peace or war for the United States, the German government did not in fact possess the power to choose peace. The Chancellor could at best only postpone the decision for war.

Director of the Wilson papers at Princeton University, ARTHUR S. LINK (1920–   ) comes to his writing on World War I through his long study of Woodrow Wilson. The most recently published volume of his massive biography takes Wilson only up to fall 1915, but Link's conclusions about the reasons for American entry can be found in his other books, chiefly *Woodrow Wilson and the Progressive Era* (1954) and *Wilson the Diplomatist* (1957) from which the essay below is drawn.*

Wilson's Struggle for Peace

Wilson's response [to the Allied rejection of his mediation offers of 1916] was a decision with momentous possibilities for good or for ill—to strengthen American neutrality and then to press forward in his own independent campaign for peace. It was the grand culmination of American neutrality and the almost inevitable outgrowth of pressures and events at home and abroad that were converging during the summer and autumn of 1916 to cause a radical shift in American foreign policy.

One of these events was Wilson's mounting anger with the British and his growing disillusionment about the merits of the whole Allied cause as a conse-quence of the British rejection (as he saw it) of his right hand of fellowship. Going far beyond mere irritation, this anger and disillusionment culminated in convictions powerful enough to affect national policy—that the Allies were fighting for selfish motives and domination, and that they would prolong the carnage rather than consent to a fair and liberal settlement.

Developments in the official relations of the United States and Great Britain during the summer and autumn of 1916 also speeded the disillusionment in Washington and prepared the way for a change of American policy. To state the matter briefly, the Admiralty and Ministry of Blockade tightened the British maritime system to the point of denying the last vestiges of the freedom of the seas. This they did by such measures as the search and seizure of American mail, carrying the economic war to America by forbidding British subjects to have any dealings with neutral individuals and firms suspected of trading with the Central Powers, and attempting to bring all American shipping under British control by denying shipmasters the right to purchase coal in distant British ports if they refused to submit to the Admiralty's control.

A force of even greater power propelling Wilson toward policies of stern neutrality and independent mediation was the extraordinary growth of American neutralism following the settlement of the *Sussex* affair. In part it was the result of a sharp increase in anti-British sentiment as a consequence of the tightening of the maritime system and the American revulsion against the ruthless way in which the British army suppressed the Irish Rebellion in April, 1916. In larger measure it was a reflection of the overwhelming desire to avoid participation in a war the outcome of which did not concern most Americans. Whatever the causes for its spectacular increase, neutralism became the reigning passion during the summer and autumn of 1916. It silenced most interventionists and destroyed politically the few (like Theodore Roosevelt) who refused to acknowledge its supremacy, invaded the national political conventions and controlled the writing of the party platforms, and made captives of both Wilson and his Republican opponent, Charles Evans Hughes, during the presidential campaign. Most important, it convinced Wilson that the vast majority of Americans would prefer to yield technically legal rights rather than to fight if Germany violated the *Sussex* pledge.

There was a final and irresistible force propelling Wilson toward a new diplomatic course at this time—his fear that the war was entering a new and more desperate stage in which the aggressions of the belligerents might drive the American people to war in sheer anger. If this happened, then Americans would be fighting in blind defense of national rights, not knowing really why they fought, and only to the end that one side might win a smashing victory and thus be able to impose a peace that could not endure. The President explained the possible dilemma poignantly in a draft of a peace note that he composed in November, 1916, but did not send:

The position of neutral nations . . . has been rendered all but intolerable. Their commerce is interrupted, their industries are checked and diverted, the lives of their people are put in constant jeopardy, they are virtually forbidden the accustomed highways of the sea. . . . If any other nation now neutral should be drawn in, it would know only that it was drawn in by some force it could not resist, because it had been hurt and saw no remedy but to risk still greater, it might be even irreparable, injury, in order to make the weight in the one scale or the other decisive; and even as a participant it would not know how far the scales must tip before the end would come or what was being weighed in the balance!

It was to avoid being caught in such a predicament as this that Wilson embarked upon the policies that I will now describe.

First, he began to move in a really menacing way to defend alleged American neutral rights in the face of the new

British maritime measures. No longer couched in friendly terms, the State Department's protests now accused the London government of "lawless" conduct and warned that the United States would not tolerate the continuation of "repeated violations of international law." To give teeth to these warnings, Wilson obtained legislation from Congress in early September empowering him to deny clearance and port facilities to ships of any nation that discriminated against American commerce, and to use the armed forces to enforce the prohibition. In addition, he persuaded the Federal Reserve Board to warn American bankers to exercise caution in financing the war trade with the Allies.

The consequences of this new sternness—a sharp increase in Anglo-American tension and vigorous protests from London—were also a calculated component of Wilson's plan. His grand objective was independent mediation, and such mediation would be possible only from a posture of severe neutrality. In other words, mediation could succeed only if the President convinced the British that he meant to use his powers of retaliation to force them to co-operate, and the Germans that he was determined to compel as much respect for American rights from their enemies as he had from them.

Wilson proceeded with his preparations for a climactic peace campaign once the voters had decreed that he should have charge of foreign relations for another four years. Protracted discussions among Wilson, Lansing, and House during late November, 1916, pointed up the possibilities and dangers of the situation. The Allies were now even more violently opposed to peace talk of any kind than they had been during the preceding

summer. The German leaders, on the other hand, were not only increasing their pressure on Wilson for a peace move, but were now even promising (at least so the German Ambassador in Washington said) to evacuate Belgium and France if the Allies consented to an armistice. There was the danger, therefore, as House and Lansing pointed out, that Germany would respond favorably to a call for peace and that the Allies would reject it. If this happened, the President's advisers further warned, then the United States might drift into a sympathetic alliance with Germany and into a naval war with England and Japan. Would it not be safer, House asked, to attempt to revive the House-Grey Agreement and to move for mediation under its terms?

These were weighty issues, and in dealing with them Wilson revealed for the first time his innermost thoughts about the war and America's duty toward the belligerents. Old plans like the House-Grey Agreement based upon the assumption of intimate Anglo-American co-operation were, he exclaimed, out of date. He must stand for peace alone, free and compelling, no matter what the risks might be. If the Germans responded favorably, he would work with them. If the Allies resisted, he would attempt to coerce them. There was the risk of a rupture and war, but he did not think that it was great.

"This morning in discussing these matters with the President," House wrote in his Diary on November 15, 1916,

he went so far as to say that if the Allies wanted war with us we would not shrink from it. . . . He thought they would not dare resort to this and if they did, they could do this country no serious hurt. I disagreed with him again. I thought Great Britain might conceivably destroy our fleet and land troops from Japan in sufficient numbers to hold certain parts of the United States. He replied they might get a good distance but would have to stop somewhere.

Neither these somber warnings, which he did not take seriously, nor the call by the German government for a peace conference, issued on December 12, diverted Wilson from the course that he had decided to pursue, and he sent a message to the belligerent capitals on December 18, 1916. In order to avoid the appearance of supporting the German maneuver, the President eliminated a demand for the assembling of a peace conference and simply asked the belligerents to say frankly what they were fighting for and upon what terms they would consent to end the war. The whole world knew, however, that it was merely the first step in a bold campaign.

The time was now at hand when the belligerent leaders had to choose between peace and prolonging the war at the risk of incurring American intervention. To provide the opportunity for frank discussions, Wilson opened secret negotiations through Colonel House with the British Ambassador in Washington, with Sir William Wiseman, an agent accredited to the British Embassy, and with the German Ambassador to the United States. While waiting for their replies, moreover, the President went before the Senate on January 22, 1917, to describe the kind of settlement that he hoped to achieve.

The British gave their answer first, on January 26, 1917, when Wiseman told House that his government would agree to the meeting of an early peace conference, provided that the Germans returned a favorable reply to the President's appeal. It was a startling announcement in view of the hitherto bitter opposition of the British Cabinet to any suggestion of mediation and the Allied public answer of January 10, 1917, to Wilson's peace note, which had revealed ambitions so sweeping that they could be realized only by the defeat of Germany. We can only guess at the reasons behind Wiseman's reply until the Foreign Office in London unseals its records for this period. By the beginning of 1917 the British almost certainly knew that the Germans had decided to begin unrestricted submarine operations in the near future. It is possible, therefore, that the leaders in London were buying Wilson's good will cheaply by giving lip service to the cause of peace in the knowledge that the United States would soon be safely in the war. It is also possible that the British had concluded that the risks of Wilsonian mediation were less than the risks of defeat through an effective submarine blockade and the disintegration of the Great Alliance, both of which now seemed ominously possible.

At this point, however, it mattered comparatively little what the British said, or why they said it. Wilson had the power of life or death over the Allies and was prepared to use it to force them to the peace table, provided that the Germans approved his objectives and accepted his leadership. As he put it:

If Germany really wants peace she can get it, and get it soon, *if she will but confide in me and let me have a chance.* . . . Feelings, exasperations are neither here nor there. Do they want me to help? I am entitled to know because I genuinely want to help and have now put myself in a position to help without favour to either side.

In the circumstances prevailing during the late autumn and early winter of 1916–1917, the Germans had three possible choices of policy. These were, first, to join hands with Wilson in a drive for peace generally on the President's terms; second, to make a limited bid for victory by intensifying the submarine war at the risk of alienating the United States; and, third, to make a supreme bid for victory by instituting a total blockade of all commerce to the British Isles. The situation from the German point of view was such that this choice would not depend upon anything that Wilson did or said, unless, of course, the President could be used as a German pawn or was willing openly to support Germany's war objectives. The German decision would depend entirely upon a realistic evaluation of the possibilities of the military situation, that is, upon whether the Imperial army and navy were capable of imposing terms upon the enemies of the Reich.

Discussions of these possibilities had begun in Germany in earnest in mid-August, 1916, as a consequence of the urgent demand of the Admiralty for permission to resume unrestricted submarine attacks in the near future. The civilian and military leaders rejected the demand at a conference at Pless Castle on August 31, 1916, on the ground that the navy did not have enough submarines to enforce a blockade and that it would obviously be foolhardy to risk American retaliation at this time. Actually, it was the new commanders of the army, Generals Paul von Hindenburg and Erich von Ludendorff, who made this decision. The military situation, they said, was too menacing to justify assuming the risk of war with America. There was heavy Allied pressure on the western front; above all, there was the grave danger of an Allied invasion of the Balkans, which might cause the collapse of Austria-Hungary.

Events of the late summer and early autumn combined inexorably to create a new situation in which a different decision would be made. First, the great British offensive on the Somme, aimed at tearing a huge hole in the German lines and a thrust into Belgium, failed; as a result, the German position in the West was again secure. Second, after dawdling in the matter for nearly two years, the Admiralty had finally launched a large program of submarine construction and the training of crews; by the end of the year it would be possible to talk in terms of dealing England a deathblow underseas. Finally, the army's counteroffensive against the Russians and its smashing victory over Rumania removed all cause for concern about the security of Austria-Hungary and the Balkans.

It was amid increasingly hopeful circumstances, therefore, that the German leaders, during November and early December, 1916, began to review their decision to hold the U-boats within the limits of the *Sussex* pledge. By this time Hindenburg and Ludendorff had concluded that the army could not break the stalemate on land and that the only hope of victory was an effective submarine blockade of the British Isles. On the other hand, the civilian leaders, particularly the Imperial Chancellor, Theobald von Bethmann-Hollweg, were still convinced that a submarine *démarche* would not only fail, but would insure Germany's ultimate defeat, because it would drive the United States to hostilities. Maneuvering within a narrowing confine of authority, the Chancellor countered with the one suggestion that offered any hope of averting a break with the United States—that the Central Powers try to end the war by negotiation. The High Command agreed, but warned that the inauguration of unrestricted submarine warfare would have to follow if the peace move failed. This, in brief, was the background of the German peace note of December 12, 1916.

As we have seen, American and German policies seemingly converged at this moment. The German leaders, even the Supreme High Command, sincerely wanted peace; the President was willing to risk his leadership and the fortunes of his country by forcing the Allies to come to a peace conference. Why, then, did what seemed almost inevitable—German-American co-operation in a peace campaign—never materialize?

The answer is not to be found by suggesting that the chief cause of the failure was Wilson's refusal to move more quickly or more forcefully. There is no reason to believe that the outcome would have been any different had the President made his peace appeal in early November or in any stronger language than he later used. The answer can be found only in a clear understanding of what the Germans hoped to gain through peace negotiations and the part that they wanted Wilson to play in the final processes.

Almost formless at the outset of the war, German war objectives had grown in a direct ratio to the progress of the Imperial armies in the field. By the late autumn of 1916 the military situation was so favorable and the potentialities of an effective submarine blockade were so great that the German leaders inevitably abandoned thought of a compromise peace and began to plan for a settlement that would remove all threats to future German security. As drawn up by Bethmann-Hollweg, amended by Hindenburg, and approved by the German and Austrian governments, the German peace terms were breath-taking in scope. They included, in the East, the establishment of a Polish kingdom under German control and German annexation of Lithuania and Courland on the Baltic; in the West, destruction of British naval supremacy, an indemnity from England and France, the annexation of strategic parts of France and Belgium, and the reconstruction of Belgium as a German vassal; and, overseas, the annexation of all or part of the Belgian Congo. To be sure, these were the maximum German objectives at the time; a realization of even part of them, however, would have secured German domination of Europe for years to come.

This was the kind of settlement that the German leaders were determined to obtain through peace negotiations. They knew that they could never obtain such terms, or even a large part of them, through Wilson's mediation. They knew that Wilson would demand, among other things, the restitution of a free and independent Belgium and perhaps the return of Alsace-Lorraine to France. Acceptance of Wilson's mediation and a compromise peace, even one based entirely upon the *status quo ante bellum*, would, in German eyes, be tantamount to defeat, for it would mean the frustration of everything for which so much German blood had been shed. As a consequence, no German leader, civilian or military, ever seriously considered accepting Wilson's *mediation*. During all the high-level discussions about peace plans, no German leader ever seriously mentioned such a possibility. On the contrary, all German diplomatic efforts were concentrated upon the goal of preventing Wilson's mediation, or "meddling," as the Germans called it.

This statement needs some clarification. The Germans were eager, almost desperately eager, to win the President's support for their peace plans. They wanted Wilson's help in forcing the Allies to the peace table at a time when all the odds favored the winning of a German peace. They were willing to give pledges of postwar disarmament and membership in a League of Nations, if this were necessary to win the President's support. But they did not want, indeed, they would not permit, Wilson's mediation or even his presence at the peace conference.

Wilson did not know these facts during the first stages of the peace discussions, but the truth finally came out in January, 1917, when the President begged the Foreign Office in Berlin to come out frankly and fully in acceptance of his mediation. Then the German leaders had to say that they would welcome Wilson's co-operation only after the peace treaty had been signed, not at the conference of belligerents itself. Shrewdly perceiving the German intentions, Wilson refused to be a pawn in Berlin's game.

Wilson's refusal meant that the German leaders would now proceed to consider means of achieving through force what they had failed to win by their inept diplomacy. The High Command had already made the decision by late December; it was confirmed by a conference of all leaders at Pless Castle on January 9, 1917. That decision was, in brief, to begin unrestricted submarine warfare against all shipping, belligerent and neutral, in the approaches to the British Isles and the eastern Mediterranean after January 31.

It was easily the most fateful decision made by any government during the course of the war, and the German records fully reveal the reasons for its adoption. It now seemed beyond all doubt that the navy had sufficient power to establish an effective submarine blockade of the British Isles, for it could send between twenty-five and thirty submarines into western waters by February 1, 1917, and a growing number after that date. Moreover, other circumstances, particularly a short wheat crop in the New World, augured well for the success of the blockade. Indeed, on a basis of elaborate calculations the Admiralty spokesmen guaranteed absolutely to reduce the British to actual starvation within five months after the submarine blockade began. If this were possible, then Germany had it within her power to win a total victory and a settlement that would establish the Reich in an unassailable position. To the military leaders, who had despaired of winning the war in the trenches, it was an opportunity that could not be refused.

Fear of American belligerency no longer had any effect on German policy in such an atmosphere of confident expectation. The German leaders all assumed that a wholesale attack on American maritime commerce would drive the United States into the war. These same leaders also concluded that American belligerency would not make any difference. On the contrary, American participation would have certain positive advantages, for it would mean the diversion of huge quantities of food and matériel to an American army in training during the very period when the U-boats would be winning the war on the seas. But in any event, American participation was in the circumstances necessary to the success of the German plans, because the submarine blockade could succeed only if it were total, that is, only if American as well as British ships were prevented from carrying life-giving supplies to the beleaguered British Isles. Of course, no German leader wanted recklessly to provoke an American declaration of war; all Germans, however, were prepared to incur American belligerency if they could win the war by so doing.

It was the only decision that seemed possible to the Imperial military commanders. No nation involved in a desperate war for survival will fail to use a weapon, whether it be the submarine or the atomic bomb, when that weapon promises to bring quick and overwhelming victory. But the submarine campaign brought catastrophic defeat to Germany and misfortunes unnumbered to the world because it destroyed all possibility of a peace of reconciliation. For this outcome, the political leaders in Berlin, particularly Chancellor Bethmann-Hollweg, were primarily responsible. Not once during the critical months of 1916 did they attempt to organize any movement for peace on a basis that could succeed. Not once did the Foreign Office make any serious effort to understand Wilson's motives and objectives. Not once during the final debates over submarine policy did the Chancellor attempt to subject the Admiralty's dubious promises to any really searching scrutiny, to determine in a realistic way what the effect of American participation would be, or to inform the Reichstag of the consequences of failure of unlimited underseas warfare. It is true that the Supreme High Command, which now had the constitutional right to override the Chancellor on submarine policy, might have proceeded as it did in any event. None the less, the fact remains that Bethmann-Hollweg simply made no serious effort to influence what was the most fateful decision confronting Germany's leaders since the formation of the Empire.[1]

There remains only one further question, whether the Germans decided to go the whole length and to attack American shipping because they believed that the United States would enter the war in any case if they violated the *Sussex* pledge. In other words, did the Germans conclude that there was little point in confining unrestricted attacks to armed merchantmen or to *belligerent* shipping, armed and unarmed, because any deviations from the rules of cruiser warfare would provoke American intervention? This is an academic question, but an important one, because the answer to it sheds additional light upon Wilson's intentions and the German choice of alternatives.

There is much evidence that by the end of 1916 Wilson was prepared to effect a sharp diplomatic withdrawal if both belligerent groups refused to heed his peace appeal. He knew that if the war proceeded the belligerents would use every means at their command to end it, and that this would mean a severe intensification of the struggle on the seas, to the further detriment of neutral rights. It seems almost certain that he would have accepted unrestricted submarine attacks against *armed* merchantmen. On January 10, 1917, the German

[1] Professor Link now thinks that his judgment of Bethmann was too severe and did not take sufficient account of the Chancellor's difficulties. —Ed.

government informed the State Department that its submarines would hereafter attack armed merchant ships without warning, because these ships had all been offensively armed and instructed to attack submarines. The German proclamation was, technically, a violation of the *Sussex* pledge,[2] but Wilson's only response was to indicate that he doubted that his earlier position on armed ships had been sound.

We can go further and say that it seems also possible that Wilson would not have broken diplomatic relations over unrestricted submarine attacks against all *belligerent* merchantmen, exclusive, perhaps, of passenger liners. Much would have depended upon American public opinion, which then seemed overwhelmingly opposed to war for the vindication of the right of Americans to travel on belligerent vessels. Much would have depended upon the President himself, but his determination to avoid participation had never been stronger than at this time. "There will be no war," he told Colonel House on January 4, 1917.

This country does not intend to become involved in this war. We are the only one of the great white nations that is free from war to-day, and it would be a crime against civilization for us to go in.

The Germans never seriously considered adopting these limited alternatives, not because they believed that any infraction of the *Sussex* pledge would automatically provoke American intervention, but because they thought that they could win only by enforcing a total

blockade.[3] But if it is true that Wilson would not have gone to war if the Germans had confined their attacks to belligerent merchantmen, then we are confronted with one of the supreme ironies of history. By doing the thing that seemed the best guarantee of victory, the Germans assured their own defeat. By failing to adopt the limited policies, they threw away their one chance of success, which might well have come after the collapse of Russia and a devastating attack on Allied commerce.

President Wilson's response to the German blockade proclamation lends additional evidence to my theory that the United States might not have broken diplomatic relations if the Germans had exempted American shipping from the wrath of their underseas campaign. The German Ambassador delivered copies of the German blockade announcement to Lansing and House on January 31, 1917. Wilson did not act like a man who had a predetermined course of action in mind. Even in the face of a German declaration of war against American commerce, he hesitated to take any step that might lead to war. He was willing, he told Lansing, to go to almost any lengths "rather than to have this nation actually involved in the conflict."

There was, however, only one decision that Wilson could now make. No great power could continue to maintain diplomatic intercourse with a government that promised to destroy its shipping and slaughter its citizens in violation of national and treaty rights and solemn

---

[2] Professor Link wishes to point out that he was in error when he wrote this sentence. The *Sussex* pledge had never covered armed ships.— Ed.

[3] The author, if he were re-writing this paragraph, would give some weight to the conviction that most German leaders held that the Allies would never consent to a negotiated peace and were bent upon destruction of the German nation.—Ed.

pledges. Small neutral states like Holland and Norway had no choice but to suffer under protest, but a great nation like the United States had responsibilities commensurate with its power and influence. Continuing to maintain relations with Berlin after the issuance of the blockade proclamation of January 31 would have meant nothing less than Wilson's condoning of the German assault upon American rights and lives. The remarkable thing is not that Wilson severed diplomatic relations as he did on February 3, but that he hesitated at all.

To engage in a debate at this point over the reasons for Wilson's severance of diplomatic relations with Germany would obscure a development that was vastly more important than the handing of passports to the German Ambassador. It was Wilson's announcement, made in an address to Congress on February 3, 1917, that the United States would accept the new submarine blockade and would not go to war, in spite of the break in relations, provided that the Germans did not carry out their threat to destroy American ships and lives. This is the clear meaning of the following paragraph in Wilson's address:

Notwithstanding this unexpected action of the German Government, . . . I refuse to believe that it is the intention of the German authorities to do in fact what they have warned us they will feel at liberty to do. I cannot bring myself to believe that they will indeed pay no regard to the ancient friendship between their people and our own or to the solemn obligations which have been exchanged between them and destroy *American ships and take the lives of American citizens* in the wilful prosecution of the ruthless naval programme they have announced their intention to adopt. Only

actual overt acts on their part can make me believe it even now.

Wilson then announced what he would do in the event that his confidence in the "sobriety and prudent foresight" of the German leaders proved unfounded:

I shall take the liberty of coming again before the Congress, to ask that authority be given me to use any means that may be necessary for the protection of our seamen and our people in the prosecution of their peaceful and legitimate errands on the high seas.

In short, Wilson was saying that he would follow a policy of watchful waiting and govern his future policies in response to what the Germans did. If they spared American ships and lives, presumably upon American ships of all categories and upon belligerent unarmed passenger vessels, then he would do nothing. If they attacked American ships, then he would defend them by an armed neutrality. This, obviously, was not the language of war, such as Lansing had urged the President to use. It was the language of a man determined to avoid such full-fledged commitment as a war declaration would imply, willing in the worst event only to protect "our seamen and our people in the prosecution of their peaceful and legitimate errands on the high seas."

Throughout the first weeks of February, 1917, the President waited patiently to see what the future would bring. At any moment the German government could have removed the possibility of war with the United States by declaring that it would respect American shipping and take all possible care to protect American lives on belligerent ships. But when the Swiss Minister in Washington offered to serve as an intermediary in any discussions between Berlin and Washington, the German Foreign Office replied that not even the re-establishment of diplomatic relations with the United States would prompt the Imperial government to reconsider "its resolution to completely stop by submarines all importations from abroad by its enemies."

In spite of the obvious German determination to enforce a total blockade, Wilson refused to permit the defense departments to make any important preparations for war. He would not do anything to cause the Germans to think that he was contemplating hostilities. As the days passed, however, the pressures for an end to watchful waiting and for the adoption of at least an armed neutrality mounted almost irresistibly. Members of the Cabinet, shipowners, a large majority of the newspapers, and a growing body of public opinion combined in the demand that the President either convoy merchantmen or arm them with naval guns and crews. Still protesting that the people wanted him to avert any risk of war, Wilson gave in to their wishes on about February 25. Going to Congress the following day to request authority to arm merchantmen and to "employ any other instrumentalities or methods that may be necessary and adequate to protect our ships and our people in their legitimate and peaceful pursuits on the seas," he carefully explained that he was not contemplating war or any steps that might lead to war. "I merely request," he said,

that you will accord me by your own vote and definite bestowal the means and the authority to safeguard in practice the right of a great people who are at peace and who are desirous of exercising none but the

rights of peace to follow the pursuits of peace in quietness and good will—rights recognized time out of mind by all the civilized nations of the world. No course of my choosing or of theirs will lead to war. War can come only by the wilful acts and aggressions of others.

Although a small group of senators prevented approval of a bill authorizing Wilson to arm merchantmen, the President took such action anyway on March 9, 1917. At the same time, he called Congress into special session for April 16, 1917, presumably in order to ask the legislative branch to sanction a more elaborate program of armed neutrality, which he set to work with his advisers in the Navy Department to devise.

By the middle of March, therefore, it seemed that Wilson had made his decision in favor of a limited defensive war on the seas. "We stand firm in armed neutrality," he declared, for example, in his second inaugural address on March 5, "since it seems that in no other way we can demonstrate what it is we insist upon and cannot forego." Yet on April 2 (he had meanwhile convened Congress for this earlier date), scarcely more than a month after he had uttered these words, he stood before Congress and asked for a declaration of full-fledged war. What events occurred, what forces were at work, what pressures were applied during this brief interval to cause Wilson to make the decision that he had been trying so desperately to avoid? We should perhaps put the question in a less positive way, as follows: What caused the President to abandon armed neutrality and to *accept* the decision for war?

There was first the fact that from the end of February to the end of March the Germans gave full evidence of their determination to press a relentless, total attack against all ships passing through the war zones that enveloped western Europe. The sinking of the British liner *Laconia* without warning on February 25 and with loss of American life, the ruthless destruction of three American merchantmen (*City of Memphis, Illinois,* and *Vigilancia*) on March 18, and the relentless attacks against the vessels of other neutral nations, to say nothing of the slashing attacks against Allied merchant shipping, removed all doubt in Wilson's mind about the deadly seriousness of the German intention to conduct total warfare against all commerce and human life within the broad war zones.

The more the character of the submarine blockade became apparent, the stronger the conviction grew in the President's mind that armed neutrality was neither a sufficient response physically, nor a proper or legally possible one. He explained this conviction in his war message:

It is a war against all nations. . . . The challenge is to all mankind. When I addressed the Congress on the 26th of February last, I thought that it would suffice to assert our neutral rights with arms, our right to use the seas against unlawful interference, our right to keep our people safe against unlawful violence. But armed neutrality, it now appears, is impracticable. Because submarines are in effect outlaws when used as the German submarines have been used against merchant shipping, it is impossible to defend ships against their attacks as the law of nations has assumed that merchantmen would defend themselves. . . . It is common prudence in such circumstances, grim necessity indeed, to endeavour to destroy them before they show their own intention. They must be dealt with upon sight, if dealt with at all. The German Government denies the right of neutrals to use arms at all within the areas of the sea which it has proscribed, even in the defense of rights which no modern publicist has ever before questioned their right to defend. The intimation is conveyed that the armed guards which we have placed on our merchant ships will be treated as beyond the pale of law and subject to be dealt with as pirates would be. Armed neutrality is ineffectual enough at best; in such circumstances and in the face of such pretensions it is worse than ineffectual; it is likely only to produce what it was meant to prevent; it is practically certain to draw us into the war without either the rights or the effectiveness of belligerents.

This passage, in my opinion, reveals the *immediate* reason why Wilson made his decision for war. It was simply that the German assault upon American lives and property was so overwhelming and so flagrant that the only possible way to cope with it was to claim the status of a belligerent in order to strike at the sources of German power. "I would be inclined to adopt . . . [armed neutrality]," the President wrote only two days before he delivered his war message,

indeed, as you know, I had already adopted it, but this is the difficulty: . . . To make even the measures of defense legitimate we must obtain the status of belligerents.

Certainly Wilson had convinced himself that this was true, but I have a strong suspicion that he would have stood doggedly by his first decision to limit American action to a defense of rights on the seas if this decision had not been overridden by convictions, events, pressures, and ambitions that were themselves decisive in Wilson's final shift from armed neutrality to war, in forcing him to the conclusion that the *immediate* circumstances left the United States with no choice but full-scale participation.

One of the most important of these factors was the subtlest and the one for which the least direct evidence can be adduced. It was Wilson's apparent fear that the threat of a German victory imperiled the balance of power and all his hopes for the future reconstruction of the world community. We must be careful here not to misinterpret his thoughts and motives. There is little evidence that he accepted the decision for war because he thought that a German victory would seriously endanger American security, because he wanted to preserve Anglo-American control of the North Atlantic sea lanes, or because he desired to maintain the traditional balance of European power because it served American interests. Nor is there any convincing evidence that Wilson's attitude toward the objectives of the rival alliances had changed by the time that he made his final decision.

On the other hand, there was now a great and decisive difference in the relative position of the belligerents: The Allies seemed about to lose the war and the Central Powers about to win it. This, almost certainly, was a governing factor in Wilson's willingness to think in terms of war. Germany, he told Colonel House, was a madman who must be curbed. A German victory meant a peace of domination and conquest; it meant the end of all of Wilson's dreams of helping to build a secure future.[4]

As the President pondered America's

---

[4] Professor Link wishes to emphasize that there is no evidence that Wilson thought that the Germans were about to win the war. He would modify the above two paragraphs if he were writing this essay in 1964, particularly by giving much greater emphasis to Wilson's conviction, shared by Colonel House, that the war was in its final stages, and American participation would not only hasten its end but also assure Wilson a large hand in making the peace.—Ed.

duty at this juncture in history, the answer must have seemed obvious to him —to accept belligerency, because now only through belligerency could the United States fulfill its mission to insure a just and lasting peace of reconciliation. This could be accomplished only by preventing a German victory and only by the assertion of such power and influence among the Allies as would come to the United States by virtue of its sacrifice of blood and treasure.

If the immediate events made a war resolution necessary, then the goal of a righteous peace was the objective that justified full-scale participation in Wilson's mind and raised that effort to a high and noble plane. It was, therefore, not war in anger that he advocated, not war sheerly in defense of national rights, but, as he put it in his war message,

[war] for democracy, for the right of those who submit to authority to have a voice in their own governments, for the rights and liberties of small nations, for a universal dominion of right by such a concert of free peoples as shall bring peace and safety to all nations and make the world itself at last free.

The combined weight of official and public opinion was another pressure meanwhile driving Wilson toward acceptance of the decision for war. It was a fact of no little consequence that by the end of March every important member of the administration, including those members of the Cabinet who had heretofore opposed any bellicose measures, urged the President to admit that a state of war with Germany in fact existed. Public opinion had remained stubbornly pacific until near the end of February, 1917. Then the publication of the Zimmermann telegram, in which the German government proposed to Mexico a war alliance against the United States, the sinking of the *Laconia,* and, above all, the destruction of American ships in the war zones after mid-March generated a demand for war that grew with mounting crescendo in all sections and among all classes, until it seemed beyond doubt to be a national and a majority demand. It was further stimulated by news of the downfall of the czarist regime and the establishment of a provisional republican government in Russia—news that convinced many wavering Americans that the Allies were indeed fighting for democracy and also changed overnight the large and influential American Jewish community from a position of strong hostility toward the Allies to one of friendship.

This was all a development of profound importance for a leader as keenly sensitive to public opinion as was Woodrow Wilson. He could have joined forces with the large antiwar minority to resist the demand for war; indeed, he probably would have done so had he been convinced that it was the wise and right thing to do. The point is not, therefore, that public opinion *forced* Wilson to accept the decision for war, but that it facilitated doing what Wilson for other reasons now thought was necessary and right to do.

All this is said without any intention of implying that Wilson ever *wanted* war. The agony of his soul was great as he moved through the dark valley of his doubts. He had no illusions about the merits of the conflict into which he and his people were being drawn. He saw the risks of intervention, both to his own nation and to the world, with remarkable clarity. But he could devise no alternative; and he set aside his doubts in the hope that acting now as a belligerent, with all the power and idealism of the American people sustaining him, he could achieve objectives to justify the misery of mankind.

WALTER LIPPMANN (1889–   ) has been for a half century one of the nation's most respected writers on public affairs. A close student of foreign affairs, more than half of his score of books deal with that subject. His article in *Life* was the first to advance the thesis that the United States entered World War I to protect its security. Because he wrote this article in spring 1941, when the threat to the country's physical security clearly was important in American policy formulation, Lippmann's critics have accused him of "present-mindedness"—attributing to an earlier generation the concerns of a later one. Is Lippmann's argument merely after-the-fact reasoning, or does he support his thesis with evidence?*

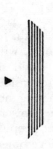

► *Security, Not Sentiment*

For the second time in 25 years the American people have intervened in a war towards which they had meant to be neutral. Their second intervention has come much more quickly than did their first one. In February 1917, when the United States broke off diplomatic relations with Germany, the Allies and the Central Powers had been fighting for 30 months; in February 1941, when Congress began to enact the Lease-Lend Bill, the war had been going on only 17 months. Yet, though the second intervention has come so much more quickly, extraordinary measures had been taken to insure American neutrality. Congress had spent years investigating the sup-posed causes of the first intervention. In 1935 and in 1936 Congress had voted and the President had signed elaborate laws designed to remove the causes which, it was believed, had brought about the intervention of 1917.

Nevertheless, after a full debate in Congress and throughout the country, neutrality has been abandoned for the second time and the United States has again intervened. We have to ask ourselves why this has happened. We must have an explanation which really does explain not only *why* we have intervened in *both* wars but why in each case we have intervened *when* we did intervene.

* Walter Lippmann, "The Atlantic and America," *Life*, April 7, 1941, pp. 85–92. Reprinted by permission of the author.

Thus it is not an explanation to say that intervention is due to bankers, munitions makers and capitalists. For while in 1917 the bankers had made loans to the Allies, in 1941 the bankers have made no loans to the Allies. In 1917 there was a great private munitions industry, and it has been said the munitions makers feared that if the Allies lost, they would be unable to keep on selling the munitions that their expanded factories were geared to produce. But in 1941 we find that American munitions makers have more American orders than they can fill and that far from having too much capacity, they have not nearly enough for our own needs alone; if Britain lost, the United States would not only continue with every British contract but would surely vastly increase its own orders as well.

Nor is it an explanation to say that we intervened the first time because Germany torpedoed our ships. For in this second war we have carefully kept our ships out of reach of the German torpedoes. Nor that we became entangled the first time because we failed to uphold our neutral rights equally against Britain and Germany. For in the second war we surrendered equally our neutral rights against Germany and Britain.

Nor is it an explanation to say that in 1917 American policy was determined by hatred of the Kaiser and Prussianism and in 1941 by hatred of Hitler and Nazism. For 30 months before we intervened in February 1917 the Kaiser was the same Kaiser. For the 17 months of this war Hitler has been the same Hitler. Nor is it an explanation to say that our action is determined by sentiment. For in the first World War, though Germany had violated Belgium, we did not intervene for 30 months, and in this war, though

Germany had violated Austria, Czechoslovakia, Denmark, Norway, the Netherlands, Belgium, Luxemburg, we still believed that we would not intervene. Nor is it an explanation to say that our actions then or now have been determined by sympathy for the oppressed. For in the first World War Germany of the Hohenzollerns was a far more liberal state than was Czarist Russia, and it was by Russia, not by Germany, that Jews and Poles were persecuted. Nor is it an explanation to say that the first time we were incited by Wilson to a crusade to make the world safe for democracy and this time by Roosevelt to a crusade to establish freedom "everywhere." For in the first war we never thought of crusading against the Russian tyranny and this time we have stood aloof from the Soviet tyranny for over 20 years, from the Fascist for nearly 20 years, from the Nazi for eight years.

None of these reasons, nor all of them together, will explain what we have to explain: why, intending to be neutral in 1914, we intervened in 1917; why, intending to be neutral in 1939, we have intervened in 1941. If we are to find the exact and genuine reason, we must explain these precise dates; if we can find the reasons which explain why in both instances we intervened *when* we intervened, we shall be justified in thinking that we know what we did in 1917 and what we are doing in 1941. And if we know that, if we really understand the two interventions, we shall, I believe, see clearly why and how we went so wrong the first time that we now have to do the work all over again a second time.

We shall find the answer, I believe, in the fact that we intervened the first time when, and only when, a victorious Germany was threatening to conquer

Britain and to become the master of the other shore of the Atlantic Ocean; that we are intervening a second time at a similar point in the war and for exactly the same fundamental reason.

Then as now, as long as the German aggression was confined within Central and Eastern Europe, the war was from the American point of view merely a European war. It was a war which, though American sympathies were aroused, did not engage the vital interests of the United States. But then, as now again, when the German aggression broke through the western defenses of Europe and invaded the Atlantic Ocean, its shores and its waters, the defenses of the United States were threatened and the American people felt that their vital interests were engaged.

In the first World War it took Germany somewhat more than two years to knock out Russia, to overrun the Balkans with the exception of Greece, to deal with Italy, and to bring France to a point where a military disaster and an internal collapse were an imminent possibility. In the winter of 1917 by its victories in the East the German army had won a free hand for an all-out assault in the West. Had that assault succeeded, it would have knocked out France and destroyed the British army. This would have given to Germany the French channel ports, and at this same period in the first war the German submarine fleet was ready, as now once more it is ready, for an attack which threatened to blockade the British Isles and to starve them into surrender.

In the second World War it took Hitler a little less than one year to reach a point in the West of Europe where he has very nearly achieved what the Kaiser was threatening to achieve in 1916–1917. The first American intervention came when the Kaiser looked as if he might conquer Great Britain and establish himself as our nearest neighbor on the other side of the Atlantic Ocean. It was to prevent this from happening, it was when America saw that this might happen, that America intervened the first time. In this second World War, the movement was much faster, the outlook has seemed more desperate. But again we began to intervene when, and only when, the British control of the Atlantic was threatened; and we have decided for an all-out support of Britain when, and only when, it had been demonstrated by the strength of the British resistance that with sufficient American aid the Atlantic Ocean could be defended by the British.

In all sorts of ways the political, the strategical and the tactical conditions of the two wars are very different. But from the American point of view they have been alike in one fundamental and controlling respect: when it was seen that Britain could not hold the other shore of the Atlantic Ocean without American help, America intervened. That is the reason why in the first war we intervened in 1917 and not in 1915 or 1916. That is why in the second war we have intervened in 1941 and not in 1939.

Though some among us deny it, though many do not clearly realize it, the great majority of Americans know by instinct and by reason that the control of the Atlantic Ocean is vital to the defense of the United States and of the whole Western Hemisphere. They know that for their physical security, for the continuation of the free way of life, it is necessary that the other shore of the Atlantic Ocean should be held by friendly and trustworthy powers. The moment it looked as if Britain might fall with France, the Congress voted almost unanimously to build another navy; no one was so pacifist, so isolationist, so little "hysterical" but that he thought that Britain's fall would require us to build the greatest naval defense in all history.

For beneath all the argument we all know that if the other shore of the Atlantic Ocean is controlled by an expanding, a conquering and an untrustworthy power, a terrible struggle to decide the mastery of the Atlantic Ocean is in the end inevitable, and that during this struggle neither the United States nor any other American republic can have peace and security.

To the generation who are too young to have known the first World War except through the cynical histories that were written after that war, it must sound strange to hear that in 1917 as in 1941 the determining cause of the American intervention was the need to defend America by preventing the conquest of the other shore of the Atlantic Ocean. They have been told about the idealism of Wilson and the hysteria of the war propaganda, and they will find it hard to believe that we intervened in 1917 as we are intervening in 1941 to support the strategical defense of the Western Hemisphere.

Yet, believe it or not, this strategical necessity was the determining cause then as now. The military and diplomatic advisers of President Wilson knew then and were moved then by the same essential estimate of America's vital interests as are Secretaries Hull, Stimson, and Knox, the advisers of President Roosevelt. If today most of us do not realize what caused the decision of 1917, the main

reason is that we have been misled about the first World War by Wilson's speeches and by historians who have never understood the war, and by politicians and propagandists who did not wish to understand it.

Yet it is the fact that we intervened in 1917 in order to defend America by aiding the Allies to defend the Atlantic Ocean against an untrustworthy and powerful conqueror. This can be proved. As proof I venture to submit excerpts from some articles which were published in February 1917 by the editors of the *New Republic*. They may be used as evidence because the journalists who wrote them had made it their business to know what was in the minds of President Wilson and of his Administration.

One of these articles, published February 17, 1917, is called "The Defense of the Atlantic World" and it states that "if the Allied fleet were in danger of destruction, if Germany had a chance of securing command of the seas, our navy ought to be joined to the British in order to prevent it. The safety of the Atlantic highway is something for which America should fight. Why? Because on the two shores of the Atlantic Ocean there has grown up a profound web of interest which joins together the western world. Britain, France, Italy, even Spain, Belgium, Holland, the Scandinavian nations, and Pan America are in the main one community in their deepest needs and their deepest purposes. They have a common interest in the ocean which unites them. They are today more inextricably bound together than most even as yet realize. But if that community were destroyed we should know what we had lost. We should understand then the meaning of the unfortified Canadian frontier, of the common protection given Latin-America by the British and American fleets.

"It is the crime of Germany that she is trying to make hideous the highways by which the Atlantic Powers live. That is what has raised us against her in this war. . . . When she carried this war to the Atlantic by violating Belgium, by invading France, by striking against Britain, and by attempting to disrupt us, neutrality of spirit or action was out of the question. And now that she is seeking to cut the vital highways of our world we can no longer stand by. . . . A victory on the high seas would be a triumph of that class which aims to make Germany the leader of the East against the West, the leader ultimately of a German-Russian-Japanese coalition against the Atlantic world."

Let the reader remember that this was written 24 years ago. Let him remember that Russia and Japan were then still the allies of Britain and France. In the light of this prophecy as to the combination which a victorious Germany would create, let him remember what has in fact happened in respect to Germany, Japan and Russia in this war. Let him then ask himself whether the men of Wilson's generation were the deluded, starry-eyed, hysterical fools that our cynical historians have taught us to think they were.

For 20 years after the Allied victory had averted the danger which Wilson foresaw, it was very easy indeed to sneer at Woodrow Wilson's demand that the world must be made safe for democracy, and sneering at it, not to understand that he saw then, as we see now, what a victory of German militarism over the sea power of the West would mean. It has taken this country 25 years to realize again what Wilson and his advisers saw

then, that "with Germany established in the position of mistress of the seas, our trade would encounter closed doors on every hand. . . . The sooner we should cancel the Monroe Doctrine the safer for us. The passing of the power of England would be calamitous to the American national interest. It is as much our concern that England should not be beaten into surrender as it was England's concern that Belgium should not be brutally trampled under. . . . (America) will be morally and politically isolated. . . . As a consequence of its isolation it will become alarmed as never before. In its fear it will arm until its territory is spotted with camps and its shores bristle with guns and battleships. . . ."

There was plenty of emotion, and even of hysteria, in 1917. But beneath it was a reasoned and statesmanlike judgment of what was vital to the defense of America, and it was this reasoning, and not the emotion and the hysteria, that moved President Wilson, the most determined pacifist that has occupied the White House since Thomas Jefferson. He did not invent this conviction of what is vital to America. The knowledge that the survival of Britain is necessary to the sure defense of America is as old as the American republic itself. Whenever Britain's survival against a continental conqueror has been in doubt, American statesmen have realized that a fundamental American interest was at stake.

Alexander Hamilton knew it in 1797 when Napoleon began his conquest of Europe: " 'Twere therefore contrary," he wrote, "to our true interest to assist in building up this colossus to the enormous size at which she aims. 'Twere a policy as short-sighted as mean to seek safety in a subserviency to her view as the price of her clemency. This at best would be but a temporary respite from the rod."

Thomas Jefferson knew it and in 1803, when Napoleon was threatening to invade England, he said: "We see with great concern the position in which Great Britain is placed, and should be sincerely afflicted were any disaster to deprive mankind of the benefit of such a bulwark against the torrent which has for some time been bearing down all before it."

We forgot these truths in the long century from 1814 to 1914 when British sea power stood unchallenged. But when it was challenged again in 1917 and 1941, Wilson and Roosevelt responded with the same fundamental conviction of American interest as had Hamilton and Jefferson before them. For the security of the Atlantic Ocean is and always has been the most fundamental American interest, and those who think this idea was invented by propagandists simply do not know American history.

But now that we are compelled for the second time in one generation to defend this vital American interest, it is indispensable that we should understand this vital interest. For the reason we have to defend it again, having won a decisive victory in 1918, is that Wilson in his public addresses became so fascinated by his vision of the future peace that he neglected to explain why America had intervened in the war. He talked of American ideals to the exclusion of American interests and thus led the country to regard as a philanthropic crusade what was in fact a defensive intervention for the preservation of American security.

Thus the nation was prevented from understanding why it had done what it did, and therefore, when the nation was victorious, it did not know how to preserve what had been won at such cost of blood and treasure. We lost the peace because we did not really remember why we had gone to war, and we shall lose this peace as well if we do not fully understand that twice we have had to intervene in Europe in order to save the British-American control of the Atlantic Ocean.

At the end of the first World War our Atlantic world had been made so safe for democracy that both here and in Great Britain the people and their politicians thought there was no need to do anything more to keep it safe for democracy. The German navy had been captured and had then scuttled itself at Scapa Flow. There were left in the Atlantic only the two great navies of Britain and the United States. The French, the Italian, and the Japanese navies were allied with the British. The English-speaking people had mastered the threat which in 1917 had compelled the United States to intervene.

Then almost immediately the English-speaking peoples, the British and ourselves, proceeded to undo what they had sacrificed so much to achieve. The British government insisted upon for herself, and assented, so far as France was concerned, to a settlement with Germany which violated the solemn contract made by President Wilson in the Armistice. The United States, partly in disgust and partly in weariness and ignorance, made a separate peace with Germany. The unworkable financial penalties imposed by the British upon Germany were matched in the United States by an unworkable debt settlement and by a tariff policy which made a sound reconstruction impossible.

The two English-speaking peoples, after they had joined together to defend their common security, broke apart. They refused to collaborate in making a tolerable peace. They refused to collaborate in revising the peace in order to make it tolerable. Each went his own separate way to the disaster which in 1928 wrecked the post-war economy. And both were so overcome by materialism and lazy shortsightedness that they let their alliances crumble and their own defenses—their own naval power—be grossly neglected.

Having separated politically, the English-speaking peoples—inspired by the good intentions which are the pavement of hell—proceeded in the name of disarmament to take the following measures:

1. The United States insisted on the rupture of the Anglo-Japanese Alliance and the isolation of Japan. This was accompanied by a policy of opposing Japanese expansion on the one hand and of dismantling our naval power on the other hand. Thus we created the situation in which the English-speaking peoples, without supreme naval power, became aligned against an isolated but expanding Japan. Instead of remaining joined with the British so that jointly we could come to terms with Japan, or jointly could oppose Japan, we separated ourselves from the British and forced them to separate themselves from Japan.

2. Insisting upon the reduction of the British and the American navies, we pushed the British into insisting, in order to maintain their relative superiority in Europe, upon a limitation of the French navy in relation to the Italian. This planted the seeds of that Anglo-French naval rivalry which produced its hideous fruits in the battle of Oran and in the menacing attitude of Admiral Darlan.

3. Throughout the 1920's the British, under the governments of MacDonald and Baldwin, ourselves in the administrations of Harding, Coolidge and Hoover, allowed our separate navies to languish. When the post-war settlement collapsed in 1929, neither country realized that a new era of world-wide disturbance had begun, and even when the disturbance produced the Nazi revolution, neither country understood how necessary it was to rebuild at once the power on which their ultimate security depends.

Thus, it was separatism, isolationism, disarmament, a blind pacifism and a mean cynicism, which in the 20 years from the Armistice to the outbreak of war reduced the English-speaking nations from a position of invincible security to that of the desperate defensive. This disintegration of Anglo-American power was the real cause of our failure to preserve the security which our first intervention achieved. It is the real cause of our having to intervene again: we are not, as some argue, repeating the error of 1917. For the defense of the security of the Atlantic world is an inexorable necessity. We are repairing the error of 1919–1920 when, having won security, we separated from Britain and thereby destroyed the means by which security had been won, by which security could alone be maintained.

This, and not the mistakes and injustices of the peace treaties, is the real reason why we are where we are today. For though the Versailles treaties were in many respect unjust, unworkable, and even dishonorable, a peaceable revision was entirely possible. By 1932, on the eve of Hitler's rise to power, German soil had already been liberated and the reparations penalties abandoned. Other revisions, even territorial revisions, were not excluded. What was lacking was power—strong enough to suppress a possible rebellion against the process of peaceable revision and adjustment and strong enough to be unafraid and, therefore, magnanimous in conciliating the vanquished.

The disintegration of the power of the English-speaking peoples destroyed the guaranties of law and order which had been created in 1918. The disintegration destroyed the will to reform the peace settlement and the capacity to enforce decisions in the post-war era. Separatism, isolationism, disarmament, pacifism and cynicism produced anarchy. They are the constituents of anarchy—of an anarchy which produced rivalry where there was need of unity, the demagogic fears of politicians where there was need of statesmanship, weakness where there had once been unchallenged power, and faint hearts where resolution was necessary. The victorious democracies of 1918 would not hang together, and so a great many of them today have already been hanged separately.

This is what has ruined the world that in 1918 we had made safe for democracy. In the 20 years between the two wars we threw away the sword and the shield which had made us victorious and secure. We forgot why we had fought. We no longer knew how we had won. We sneered at the faith that had saved us once and must be humbly reconstituted if we are to be saved again.

When we have understood why we intervened the first time, how we failed to maintain our victory, and why we are compelled to intervene again, there will be no mystery as to what must be the war aims of the English-speaking peoples or what must be the plan of the next peace. We intervened the first time in

order to preserve for the English-speaking peoples the command of the Atlantic Ocean: for a century the nations, from Scandinavia to the Argentine, which face the Atlantic Ocean have had an unparalleled opportunity to develop in freedom. Under the protection of sea power in the hands of free governments the shores and the waters of the Atlantic have been the geographical center of human liberty. We lost the peace because we let the protecting and regulating sea power of the English-speaking peoples disintegrate. We are compelled to intervene a second time in order to stop this disintegration from producing an irreparable catastrophe.

The basic war aim of the English-speaking peoples must, therefore, be to vindicate their sea power against the assault which is launched against it. Had they preserved the collaboration which won the other war, had they maintained their joint power, the assault would probably never have been launched. Had they been more nearly ready to resist when the attack was launched, they would have defended the Atlantic world on the Rhine and not, as today, over England and Scotland and Wales and in the ocean from Ireland to Brazil. What war aim can they have except to repel and defeat the assault, to raise up again the French, the Belgians, the Dutch, the Norwegians, the Czechs who stood in the first line of their defense, and then to achieve an armistice in which the free peoples—led and supported by the British and the Americans—will again be free to shape the future of the world?

And what can be our basic aim in the peace settlement except to establish firmly this time what we should never have lost the last time: a firm, enduring partnership in world affairs among the English-speaking peoples. . . .

GEORGE F. KENNAN (1904–   ) is probably America's best known career diplomat. His nearly thirty years of service include assignments as ambassador to the U.S.S.R. and Yugoslavia and as director of the Policy Planning Staff of the Department of State during the crucial years after World War II. He has spent most of the past decade in academic life, publishing several scholarly studies on Russian-American relations in the World War I period. In this essay Kennan, a critic of the moralistic-legalistic approach to foreign policy, points to alternative policies that might have been pursued during 1914–1917. Since he attributes American entry to a misplaced sentimental attachment to neutral rights, he is by inference at odds with Lippmann's conclusions.*

The Realist Position

With respect to the origins of the war: let us note that there was for long no understanding in this country that either the origins or the issues of the war were of any concern to us. Speaking in 1916, President Wilson said that with the objects and causes of the war "we are not concerned. The obscure foundations from which its stupendous flood has burst forth we are not interested to search for or explore." "America," he said on a later occasion, "did not at first see the full meaning of the war. It looked like a natural raking out of the pent-up jealousies and rivalries of the complicated politics of Europe." Here, we may note, there was no recognition that what might be at issue in the European war was anything that concerned us. There was the same denial we saw in the case of the Far East—of the legitimacy of the real interests and aspirations of other peoples, the same dismissal of these things as unsubstantial and unworthy of our attention, as "jealousies and rivalries" too silly, too "complicated," to deserve our respect.

Proceeding on this basis, it was logical that the only American interest in the war we were inclined to recognize for a long time was the defense of our neutral rights according to the established laws of maritime warfare, as they had been known in the past. We did not under-

* Reprinted from *American Diplomacy, 1900–1950* by George F. Kennan, by permission of The University of Chicago Press. Copyright 1951 by The University of Chicago. Pp. 64–73.

stand that new modalities of warfare and new weapons—above all, the total blockade and the submarine—had rendered obsolete some of the more important of these rules. Not only had their observance become physically impracticable, but each side had come to feel that its chances of victory and survival depended on the violation of one or another of them. Either side would have preferred to accept war with us rather than refrain from violating certain ones of them. This meant that a strict insistence by us on their observance could eventually lead us, theoretically, into war with both belligerents—a paradoxical ending for a policy designed to keep us out of war.

Looking backward today on these endless disputes between our government and the belligerents over neutral rights, it seems hard to understand how we could have attached so much importance to them. They irritated both belligerents and burdened our relations with them, and I find it hard to believe that they involved our national honor. It might be our privilege to defend the rights of our citizens to travel on belligerent vessels, but it was hardly a duty, unless we chose to define it as a duty to ourselves.

As time went on, there grew up, of course, alongside this outlook, something quite different: a realization of the danger of defeat that confronted the Entente powers and an awareness of the damage that would be done to our world position by the elimination of England as a strong force in the world. In addition to this, the superiority of British propaganda, and other factors, began to work to the benefit of the Allied cause. The result was a gradual growth of pro-Allied sentiment, and particularly in the minds of the responsible American leaders. This sentiment was enough to cause Wilson and House to water down our neutrality policy to the benefit of the British and to make cautious efforts to stop the war, in 1915 and 1916, as the best means of averting the danger of a British defeat. But this pro-Ally feeling was never sufficient to constitute, for the national consciousness as a whole, adequate justification for entering the war; and you will remember that our entry, when it came, was over an issue of neutrality.

Once in the war, we had no difficulty in discovering—and lost no time in doing so—that the issues involved in it were of the greatest significance to us.

It is surely a curious characteristic of democracy: this amazing ability to shift gears overnight in one's ideological attitudes, depending on whether one considers one's self at war or at peace. Day before yesterday, let us say, the issues at stake between ourselves and another power were not worth the life of a single American boy. Today, nothing else counts at all; our cause is holy; the cost is no consideration; violence must know no limitations short of unconditional surrender.

Now I know the answer to this one. A democracy is peace-loving. It does not like to go to war. It is slow to rise to provocation. When it has once been provoked to the point where it must grasp the sword, it does not easily forgive its adversary for having produced this situation. The fact of the provocation then becomes itself the issue. Democracy fights in anger—it fights for the very reason that it was forced to go to war. It fights to punish the power that was rash enough and hostile enough to provoke it—to teach that power a lesson it will not forget, to prevent the thing from happening again. Such a war must be carried to the bitter end.

This is true enough, and if nations could afford to operate in the moral climate of individual ethics, it would be understandable and acceptable. But I sometimes wonder whether in this respect a democracy is not uncomfortably similar to one of those prehistoric monsters with a body as long as this room and a brain the size of a pin: he lies there in his comfortable primeval mud and pays little attention to his environment; he is slow to wrath—in fact, you practically have to whack his tail off to make him aware that his interests are being disturbed; but, once he grasps this, he lays about him with such blind determination that he not only destroys his adversary but largely wrecks his native habitat. You wonder whether it would not have been wiser for him to have taken a little more interest in what was going on at an earlier date and to have seen whether he could not have prevented some of these situations from arising instead of proceeding from an undiscriminating indifference to a holy wrath equally undiscriminating.

In any case, once we were at war, it did not appear to us that our greatest danger might still lie precisely in too long a continuation of the war, in the destruction of Europe's equilibrium, and in the sapping of the vital energies of the European peoples. It did not appear to us then that the greatest interest we had in the war was still that it should be brought to an end as soon as possible on a basis involving a minimum maladjustment and as much stability as possible for the future. Prior to our entry into the war, many people had thought that way. As late as January, 1917, Wilson was still arguing against total victory. A

"peace forced upon the loser, a victor's terms imposed upon the vanquished," he said, "would be accepted in humiliation, under duress, at an intolerable sacrifice, and would leave a sting, a resentment, a bitter memory upon which terms of peace would rest . . . as upon quicksand." But, once we were in the war, these ideas were swept away by the powerful currents of war psychology. We were then as strong as anybody else in our determination that the war should be fought to the finish of a total victory.

Considerations of the power balance argued against total victory. Perhaps it was for this very reason that people in this country rejected them so emphatically and sought more sweeping and grandiose objectives, for the accomplishment of which total victory could plausibly be represented as absolutely essential. In any case, a line of thought grew up, under Wilson's leadership, which provided both rationale and objective for our part in fighting the war to a bitter end. Germany was militaristic and antidemocratic. The Allies were fighting to make the world safe for democracy. Prussian militarism had to be destroyed to make way for the sort of peace we wanted. This peace would not be based on the old balance of power. Who, as Wilson said, could guarantee equilibrium under such a system? It would be based this time on a "community of power," on "an organized common peace," on a League of Nations which would mobilize the conscience and power of mankind against aggression. Autocratic government would be done away with. Peoples would themselves choose the sovereignty under which they wished to reside. Poland would achieve her independence, as would likewise the restless peoples of the Austro-

Hungarian Empire. There would be open diplomacy this time; peoples, not governments, would run things. Armaments would be reduced by mutual agreement. The peace would be just and secure.

In the name of such principles you could fight a war to the end. A future so brilliant would surely wash away the follies and brutalities of the war, redress its injuries, heal the wounds it had left. This theory gave us justification both for continuing the war to its bitter and terrible end . . . and at the same time for refusing to preoccupy ourselves with the practical problems and maladjustments to which the course of hostilities was leading. Under the protecting shadow of this theory, the guns continued their terrible work for a final year and a half after our entry. Under the shadow of this theory Wilson went to Versailles unprepared to face the sordid but all-important details of the day of reckoning. Under this theory he suffered his tragic and historic failure. Under this theory things advanced with a deadly logic and precision to a peace which was indeed "forced upon the loser, a victor's terms imposed upon the vanquished, accepted in humiliation, under duress"—a peace that did indeed leave a sting, a resentment, a bitter memory, and upon which its own terms came later to rest "as upon quicksand."

And the tragedy of this outcome was not substantially mitigated by the fact that we were not signatories to the Treaty of Versailles and kept ourselves aloof from its punitive provisions. The damage had been done. The equilibrium of Europe had been shattered. Austria-Hungary was gone. There was nothing effective to take its place. Germany, smarting from the sting of defeat and plunged into profound social unrest by the breakup of her traditional institutions, was left nevertheless as the only great united state in Central Europe. Russia was no longer there, as a possible reliable ally, to help France contain German power. From the Russian plain there leered a single hostile eye, skeptical of Europe's values, rejoicing at all Europe's misfortunes, ready to collaborate solely for the final destruction of her spirit and her pride. Between Russia and Germany were only the pathetic new states of eastern and Central Europe, lacking in domestic stability and the traditions of statesmanship—their peoples bewildered, uncertain, vacillating between brashness and timidity in the exercise of the unaccustomed responsibilities of independence. And to the other side of Germany were France and England, reeling, themselves, from the vicissitudes of the war, wounded far more deeply than they themselves realized, the plume of their manhood gone, their world positions shaken.

Truly, this was a peace which had the tragedies of the future written into it as by the devil's own hand. It was a peace, as the French historian Bainville said, which was too mild for the hardships it contained. And this was the sort of peace you got when you allowed war hysteria and impractical idealism to lie down together in your mind, like the lion and the lamb; when you indulged yourself in the colossal conceit of thinking that you could suddenly make international life over into what you believed to be your own image; when you dismissed the past with contempt, rejected the relevance of the past to the future, and refused to occupy yourself with the real problems that a study of the past would suggest.

But suppose you hadn't taken this line. Would things have been different? Was there another line you could take?

It does seem to me there was.

You might have begun, I should think, with a recognition of the importance to us of what was brewing in Europe in those years before the outbreak of war. You will remember that Wilson dismissed all this as something we were not even interested to examine.

Yet, was it all so silly, so unworthy of attention? I said in the beginning that some of the causes of the war were deep ones. The absence of a major war on the Continent during the century before 1914 had rested on a balance of power which presupposed the existence of France, Germany, Austria-Hungary, and Russia as dominant elements—and all of this flanked by an England instinctively conscious of her stake in the preservation of the balance among them and prepared to hover vigilantly about the fringes of the Continent, tending its equilibrium as one might tend a garden, yet always with due regard for the preservation of her own maritime supremacy and the protection of her overseas empire. In this complicated structure lay concealed not only the peace of Europe but also the security of the United States. Whatever affected it was bound to affect us. And all through the latter part of the nineteenth century things were happening which *were* bound to affect it: primarily the gradual shift of power from Austria-Hungary to Germany. This was particularly important because Austria-Hungary had not had much chance of becoming a naval and commercial rival to England, whereas Germany definitely did have such a chance and was foolish enough to exploit it aggressively, with a chip on her shoulder, in a way that gave

the British a deep sense of concern and insecurity.

It is not only in retrospect that these things are visible.

In the winter of 1913 there appeared, anonymously, and in an English magazine (because no American magazine would take it), an article written by an American diplomatist of the time, Mr. Lewis Einstein. In this article, Mr. Einstein drew attention to the storm clouds gathering over Europe, to the depth of the Anglo-German antagonism, to the danger that war might arise from some relatively insignificant incident, and to the effect that such a war might have on the equilibrium and stability of Europe. He then went on to trace out the significance of such a European war for the security of the United States. He never doubted that we would have to intervene to save England, if the alternative were clearly her destruction. But he warned against the assumption that we would not be affected by any drastic alteration either way in the balance of forces in Europe:

Unperceived by many Americans, the European balance of power is a political necessity which can alone sanction on the Western Hemisphere the continuance of an economic development unhandicapped by the burden of extensive armaments.
. . . The disappearance or diminution of any one state in Europe would be a calamity, varying with its degree. . . .

It is no affair of the United States even though England were defeated, so long as the general balance is preserved. But if ever decisive results are about to be registered of a nature calculated to upset what has for centuries been the recognized political fabric of Europe, America can remain indifferent thereto only at its own eventual cost. If it then neglects to observe that the interests of the nations crushed are likewise its own,

America will be guilty of political blindness which it will later rue.

Now you could, it seems to me, have taken this view—so well substantiated by the subsequent course of events—as your point of departure, let us say, from 1913. You might then, departing from the recognition that serious troubles *were* brewing in Europe and that our own interests *were* endangered, have seen to it that this country provided itself right then and there with something in the way of an armed establishment, so that our word would carry some weight and be listened to in the councils of the powers. When war broke out, you could have ignored the nonsensical timidities of technical neutrality and used our influence to achieve the earliest possible termination of a war that nobody could really win. Admittedly, if there were any possibility of this, it was in the first months of the war, and we would have had to be armed. If this had not succeeded, then you would have had to carry on through the war, exercising what moderating influence you could, avoiding friction with the belligerents on minor matters, holding your power in reserve for the things that counted. And if you finally had to intervene to save the British from final defeat (which I am quite prepared to accept as a valid ground for intervention), then you could have gone in frankly for the avowed purpose both of doing this and of ending the war as rapidly as possible; you could have refrained from moralistic slogans, refrained from picturing your effort as a crusade, kept open your lines of negotiation to the enemy, declined to break up his empires and overthrow his political system, avoided commitments to the extremist war aims of your allies,

retained your freedom of action, exploited your bargaining power flexibly with a view to bringing its full weight to bear at the crucial moments in order to achieve the termination of hostilities with a minimum prejudice to the future stability of the Continent.

All these things, as I say, you might conceivably have done. If you ask me, "Can you guarantee that this would have produced a better outcome and a happier future?" my answer is, "Of course not." I can say only that I fail to see how it could have produced a much worse one. And I can say that it would have been a conceptual framework more closely related to the realities of the world we live in and that in the long run—in the law of averages—conduct realistically motivated is likely to be more effective than conduct unrealistically motivated.

But I think I hear one great, and even indignant, objection to what I have suggested; and I must speak to it before I close. People will say to me: You know that what you have suggested was totally impossible from the standpoint of public opinion; that people in general had no idea that our interests were affected by what was going on in Europe in 1913; that they would never have dreamed of spending real money for armaments in time of peace; that they would never have gone into a war deliberately, as a result of cold calculation about the balance of power elsewhere; that they would have made war only upon direct provocation; that they could never have been brought to forgive such provocation and to refrain from pressing such a war to its final conclusion. And you know that they would not have been happy unless they had been able to clothe their military effort in the language of idealism and to persuade themselves that anything so important as Americans fighting on foreign soil had to end with a basic alteration of the terms of life among nations and a settlement of this business for once and for all. You—these people will say to me—hold yourself out as a realist, and yet none of these things you are talking about were even ever within the realm of practical possibility from the standpoint of domestic realities in our own country.

I have no quarrel with this argument. I am even going to concede it. I do think that political leaders might have made greater efforts than they did, from time to time, to inform themselves and to tell people the true facts, and I think people might even have understood them and been grateful to them if they had. But let us let that go and say that basically the argument is sound. I still have one thing to say about it.

I am not talking here about the behavior of Woodrow Wilson or Colonel House or Robert Lansing. I am talking about the behavior of the United States of America. History does not forgive us our national mistakes because they are explicable in terms of our domestic politics. If you say that mistakes of the past were unavoidable because of our domestic predilections and habits of thought, you are saying that what stopped us from being more effective than we were was democracy, as practiced in this country. And, if that is true, let us recognize it and measure the full seriousness of it—and find something to do about it. A nation which excuses its own failures by the sacred untouchableness of its own habits can excuse itself into complete disaster. . . . The margin in which it is given to us to commit blunders has been drastically narrowed in the last fifty years. If it was the workings of our democracy that were inadequate in the past, let us say so. Whoever thinks the future is going to be easier than the past is certainly mad. And the system under which we are going to have to continue to conduct foreign policy is, I hope and pray, the system of democracy.

If Kennan differs with Lippmann on his security thesis inferentially, ROBERT E. OSGOOD (1921–   ) takes issue with him explicitly. A political scientist at the University of Chicago and author of *Limited War; the Challenge to American Strategy* (1957) and *NATO; The Entangling Alliance* (1962), Osgood began his examination of the Lippmann argument while still a graduate student. In this selection, he measures that thesis against the historical evidence and concludes that it is unfounded. Before making your own final judgment on the validity of the security thesis, it would be helpful to reread the latter parts of the previous selections by Buehrig and Link.*

Sentiment, Not Security

Leaving aside the nuances of Lippmann's thesis, one might fairly paraphrase it in the following manner:

The predominant American interest in the European war, the interest which the nation could least afford to forfeit, was its own self-defense, which depended upon the securing of the Atlantic Community through the defeat of Germany. By April, 1917, certain conditions, particularly submarine warfare, confronted America with the alternative of either entering the war on the side of the Allies or else jeopardizing its predominant interest. The majority of the American people understood this alternative intuitively, and many perceived it clearly. Because of this understanding and perception the United States intervened.

This is a plausible explanation of American intervention. . . . At the turn of the century and afterward, a number of leaders as well as observers of American foreign policy had concluded that America's fundamental strategic interest lay in the continued predominance of the British Navy athwart the vital lines of communication leading into the Atlantic and in the preservation of a European balance of power to prevent an aggressive Germany from gaining continental hegemony. And with this configuration of national interest in mind, many had warily speculated upon the threat to American security which might follow a relative decrease of British

* Reprinted from *Ideals and Self-Interest in America's Foreign Relations* by Robert E. Osgood, by permission of The University of Chicago Press. Copyright 1953 by The University of Chicago, Pp. 116–117, 134, 172–175, 195–197, 221–226, 261–263.

power or an increase of German power. True, this consideration had failed to impress itself upon the general public; but if, in the course of a world war, the hypothetical circumstances which such calculations anticipated were actually to materialize, then the clear threat to national self-preservation might yet induce a widespread awareness of basic strategic interests and generate a popular determination to protect them, even at the cost of intervention.

The plausibility of Lippmann's thesis is enhanced by the fact that its view of America's interest in a British victory was actually espoused by a good many Americans while the nation was in the throes of neutrality. As Lippmann indicated in *U.S. Foreign Policy,* he was himself one of those who insisted upon a realistic appraisal of the effect of a German victory upon America's security. . . .

Whether this potential source of realism became an actual source is quite a different question. If the thesis is correct that the United States intervened in the war primarily upon a calculation of its own security, that would suggest that by April, 1917, a realistic approach to world politics exerted considerable influence upon the nation. But the thesis is by no means verified by the fear which a number of citizens felt and urged concerning the consequences of a German victory, even though, as in the case of Lippmann, this fear may have been a dominant consideration at the time of intervention. In the eventful years between the summer of 1914 and the spring of 1917 the American people were assaulted by many powerful appeals; in the light of the evolution of the American attitude toward international relations since the war with Spain, it would seem likely that the general public's response was governed by many factors besides the appeal to national self-preservation. . . .

Even if it were true that a number of high officials and advisers to the administration favored America's entrance into the war primarily in order to redress the balance of power and to safeguard the Atlantic lines of communication, it would not follow that their views were a decisive cause of American intervention. That is quite another proposition.

The influence of these men upon the course of the nation during 1914–17 would be difficult to determine with any assurance. However, it is reasonable to assume that a major share of their influence would have had to be transmitted through the thoughts and actions of the nation's Chief Executive, for no President was ever in more complete control of the conduct of the nation's foreign affairs than Woodrow Wilson. Therefore, it is pertinent to inquire about the relation of the President to his advisers.

In the broad outlines of his foreign policy and the principal decisions implementing it, Wilson was remarkably independent of his advisers. These men have testified to their inability to change the President's mind upon important issues. Partly because of his innate stubbornness but largely because of his steadfast resolve to make scholarly and impartial decisions, Wilson was extremely cautious and deliberate in forming his opinions and quite tenacious of them once they were formed. He might listen patiently to a variety of advice, and he often appeared to accept the views of others without question; but because he tended to lose confidence in those who differed with him very often, most members of his cabinet were careful not to dissent too frequently, lest they lose what influence they had; and on crucial issues his seemingly unquestioning acceptance of the views of others was more the pose of impartiality than the reality of acquiescence.

As a matter of fact, Wilson's independence was strongest when the most important issues were at stake, for then he felt the full weight of his responsibility for resolving crises with wise and exalted decisions. Thus when he composed his note of protest over the sinking of the *Lusitania,* he avoided consulting anyone, even the experts of the State Department. When he had completed the draft on his own typewriter, as was his custom, he submitted it to the cabinet, and on May 13 the note was sent to Germany practically as originally drafted.

On numerous occasions Wilson rejected the counsel of his chief advisers when they advocated a tougher stand against Germany or a softer policy toward Great Britain. His distrust of this kind of advice increased as America's relations with Germany grew more critical. He came to regard Ambassador Page as so biased that he refused to read his letters. He was at odds with almost all his advisers during the weeks immediately preceding the severing of diplomatic relations with Germany, since his determination to secure peace between the belligerents was never greater than at that time.

Among all his advisers, the President probably relied most heavily upon the opinions of Colonel House. Although House's papers exaggerate his influence upon the Chief Executive, it is true that

Wilson shared many of House's views on international relations. Wilson felt such a deep friendship for his confidant that he was wont to refer to him as an extension of his own personality. When House was in England seeking American mediation, Wilson wrote, "I am of course content to be guided by your judgment as to each step." It was on the assumption that his intimate friend completely understood his mind and agreed with his judgments that Wilson trustingly delegated the solution of such important problems to him.

However, Wilson's trust in House was not always accompanied by a frank meeting of minds. Consequently, it led to some significant misunderstandings—as, for example, over the purposes and terms of American mediation—which left a residue of distrust that could never be dispelled. Wilson was, at times, willing to give his alter ego full rein in exploring possibilities and opening discussions and negotiations; but he never accepted from House or anyone else a concrete and detailed proposal in final form without subjecting it to the scrutiny of his own intellect. Eventually, when Wilson was forced to think out certain vital issues for himself, the assumption that House's mind was as one with his own could no longer be reconciled with his own opinions.

The final word on Wilson's independence was delivered by Secretary of Interior Lane.

My own ability to help him is very limited, for he is one of those men made by nature to tread the winepress alone. The opportunity comes now and then to give a suggestion or to utter a word of warning, but on the whole I feel that he probably is less dependent upon others than any President of our time. He is conscious of public sentiment—surprisingly so—for a man who sees comparatively few people, and yet he never takes public sentiment as offering a solution for a difficulty; if he can think the thing through and arrive at the point where public sentiment supports him, so much the better.

President Wilson's official biographer, Ray Stannard Baker, has concluded that Wilson "personally dominated, as the head of no other nation perhaps dominated, the international relations of the country." If this is true, the key to American intervention must lie in the thoughts and actions of the Chief Executive more than in the purposes of any other individual or group of individuals.

Before the war in Europe broke out Wilson had demonstrated, especially in his policy toward Latin America, his profound dedication to America's mission of bringing constitutional and democratic liberty, universal peace, and the Golden Rule to all the peoples of the world. He had proclaimed that Americans were placed on earth as mankind's shining example of the subordination of material and national interests to the highest moral values and the service of humanity. By 1914 Wilson had formulated and had begun to put into practice certain ideal principles of American foreign policy. On the other hand, he had given very little thought to problems of national security and the exigencies of power politics. And as for the balance of power, he abhorred it as a tool of militarists and despots.

Wilson was not blind to America's strategic interests. His policy toward Mexico, Nicaragua, San Domingo, Haiti, and Latin America in general, like the hemispheric policy of his predecessors in office, was motivated, in part, by a desire to safeguard American security by keep-ing the Western Hemisphere free from opportunities for European interference. Moreover, he seems to have believed at one time that the nation's hemispheric defense would be jeopardized by a German victory in the European war. The British ambassador Spring-Rice, in a letter to Sir Edward Grey early in September, 1914, reported a conversation with the President in which Wilson expressed the opinion that if Prussian militarism won the war, the United States would have to take such measures of defense as would be fatal to its form of government and its ideals. Harley Notter, in a studious examination of the philosophical bases of Wilson's foreign policy, has said that, undoubtedly, an "impelling consideration" in Wilson's desire to purchase the Danish West Indies was the threat to the Monroe Doctrine which would follow transfer of the islands to a Germany victorious in Europe; and that the "dominant factor" in Wilson's policy toward these islands was the general protection of the Canal and America's strategic interests in the Caribbean.

Yet Wilson's private correspondence contains only a hint here and there of any fear of the impact of a German victory upon America's position in world politics, while his public pronouncements are almost totally devoid of strategic considerations. Moreover, on numerous occasions he specifically disavowed the existence of any German threat to the national security. For example, Colonel House records Wilson's opinion in the fall of 1914 that "even if Germany won, she would not be in a condition seriously to menace our country for many years to come. . . . He did not believe there was the slightest danger to this country from foreign invasion, even if the Germans were successful."

After the first half-year of the war Wilson steadfastly maintained that, no matter which side won, the warring nations of the world would be so utterly exhausted that, for a generation at least, they could not possibly threaten the United States, even economically; but that, on the contrary, they would desperately need America's healing influence.

Those who had direct access to the President during the neutrality years have testified to their inability to impress upon him the gravity of the German threat. Thus Lansing in a memorandum to himself early in the summer of 1916 expressed his amazement at Wilson's inability to grasp the real issues of the war: "That German imperialistic ambitions threaten free institutions everywhere apparently has not sunk very deeply into his mind. For six months I have talked about the struggle between Autocracy and Democracy, but do not see that I have made any great impression."

Actually, Wilson was impressed by the struggle between autocracy and democracy; and, eventually, in his War Message he placed American might on the side of democracy; but, far from implying the preservation of a balance of power, as Lansing hoped, Wilson's pronouncement heralded the death of this iniquitous system and the birth of a new order in international relations, in which power politics and the pursuit of selfish national interests would be supplanted by the higher moral standards of personal conduct. In fact, Wilson's conception of foreign relations was remarkable not so much for its neglect of the problems of power as for its conscious subordination of national expediency to ideal goals. Above all, he coveted for America the distinction of a nation transcending its own selfish interests and dedicated in altruistic service to humanity. . . .

Woodrow Wilson led the United States into war with the same altruistic passion that had pervaded his policy of neutrality. Although he failed to resolve the inconsistencies and incongruities of the nation's strict stand upon its neutral rights, he surmounted them, in his own mind, by fixing his vision upon the transcendent objectives of the American mission. Although he reached his final decision with great reluctance, he reached it with no lack of conviction or determination; nor was he troubled with gnawing doubts as to its present justification and ultimate vindication. But what of the nation as a whole? Did Woodrow Wilson speak the public mind? For what ends and with what motives did the American people enter the war?

From the standpoint of winning the war it probably made little difference whether Americans entered it to redress the balance of power, to vindicate their honor and rights, to make the world safe for democracy, or to achieve a democratic association of nations. But the public's motives made a vast difference as far as the aftermath of war was concerned, for the effect of America's participation upon its postwar role in world politics was, in large measure, determined by the reasons for which the nation intervened and fought.

America's intervention in World War I came not as an exhilarating breath of Manifest Destiny but rather as the sigh of exasperation punctuating a reluctant conclusion. The crusade of 1898, compared to its successor of 1917, had come naturally and painlessly. Its consequences, though they had seemed revolutionary to some and shocking to others, were very quickly reconciled with the popular attitude toward international relations. Those who felt that the crusade had been perverted were consoled by new vistas for the American mission revealed by the nation's ascendance to world-wide power and prestige. The war with Spain, though variously interpreted, was readily accepted as an inevitable stage of American progress. But World War I came to America from across the sea as an aberration of international society. Intervention came, not spontaneously, but in the wake of hesitations and doubts.

In the aftermath of World War I it became gradually more difficult for Americans to reconcile their intervention with their conception of America's proper role in world politics. As they measured their experience against traditional attitudes, Americans, inevitably, drew a comparison between the reasons for intervention and its consequences; and the results of that comparison deeply affected their adjustment to the international environment.

This phenomenon is inexplicable except in terms of America's international innocence. When war became a fact to Europeans, it had become an anachronism to Americans. Until then the twentieth century had seemed like a happy continuation of the nineteenth; in other words, a beneficent era of material and cultural progress and the growth of international harmony and understanding, a wholly enlightened era of universal suffrage, international arbitration, equal rights, peace congresses, social legislation, and cooling-off treaties. A glow of great expectations lighted American skies, and the tender blossoms of domestic and international reform sweetened the air. In 1914 Andrew Carnegie and Nicholas Murray Butler were thinking about war in terms of peace palaces.

A people in such a pacific mood as this could not easily embrace war. Yet a people so proud would not pay the price of peace. A few years of neutrality demonstrated that moral optimism and the love of peace were no guarantee that peace would prevail. A few years of victory proved that America's choice of war had brought no clear assurance of the wisdom of intervention. It was this latter situation that revealed the true significance of the nation's reasons for its fateful decision.

For a nation so confirmed in peace and nonintervention as America only the most convincing and enduring reasons could have seemed valid in the aftermath of war. In hindsight, it seems that, given the circumstances after the war, only those reasons, only those ends and motives, which were of compelling national interest and which victory could have assured would have appeared worth the price of America's involvement in a European conflict. Self-defense might have been such an end, if the nation's security had been clearly threatened. The vindication of national honor was intangible and less convincing or enduring. Certainly, altruistic service to humanity was the most difficult of all ends to pursue or to achieve through warfare.

Obviously, the considerations which lead a people to undertake a war are seldom precise or rigidly logical. There is no attempt here to present a comprehensive analysis of the public's complex motivation. But self-defense, the national honor, and service to humanity are singled out because the way in which millions of American citizens responded to these ends holds a vital clue to the significance of that momentous experience in the nation's adaptation to its international environment.

This chapter is concerned with the

first objective, self-defense, and, more particularly, with the preparedness movement, which led to unprecedented peacetime defense measures, since that movement relates so closely to the nation's attitude toward its security. If there is truth in Lippmann's thesis that the American people supported intervention because they intuitively understood that their self-preservation would be threatened by Germany's domination of the opposite shore of the Atlantic, one would expect to find evidence of this intuition in the evolution of the preparedness movement. . . .

Although no issue would seem to have concerned American security more directly than the issue of military preparation for defense, the preparedness movement, in reality, conspicuously failed to produce a dispassionate and realistic discussion of the fundamental bases of national self-preservation. It failed, fundamentally, because the circumstances of the war did not arouse any serious or widespread doubt about America's impregnable physical isolation and because they *did* arouse a strong concern for the nation's honor and self-respect. In general, the preparedness movement reflected the same sentiments, anxieties, ambitions, and uncertainties that characterized America's whole reluctant but steady drift into war. If Germany had seemed likely to win the war, if the British Navy had been crushed and the Continent of Europe overrun, perhaps then the preparedness movement would have constituted an education in the exigencies of power politics and survival; but, as it was, the movement actually amounted to miseducation, for, in deference to traditional American attitudes, both sides in the argument presented national security as something the na-

tion could achieve, quite apart from its overall political policies and their relation to the stream of world politics, by arming a metaphorical fortress to resist an hypothetical assault. If the preparedness movement had any effect upon America's sense of security, it probably strengthened it, for the unprecedented defense measures that Congress finally adopted seemed to guarantee the invulnerability of the national fortress, even against the most powerful assailant.

There was little in the way America prepared militarily to indicate that she was prepared psychologically to assume the burden of intervention in a war so irrelevant to the instinct of self-preservation. . . .

The development of the preparedness movement suggests that the circumstances of the European conflict had more effect on American public opinion than all the millions of words spent upon the question. The argument that a victorious Germany might invade the Western Hemisphere was bound to seem implausible when Germany was unable to conquer France and England. But the tragic sinking of the *Lusitania* was an incontrovertible fact. The American people would prepare to fight for their rights, but as for the threat to their security, they adopted a "show me" attitude.

Germany's submarine warfare might, nevertheless, have aroused the instinct of self-preservation which Lippmann perceived in retrospect, if the American people had been truly conditioned by their experience in world politics to respond to threats to the Atlantic Community. But that, distinctly, was not the case, for the great body of the nation had never known the fear of insecurity; it had not been touched by the discipline of adversity. Consequently, Americans approached the war in Europe with no familiar perspective of national interest, except the traditional policies of neutrality and nonintervention, which were based upon the assumption that the United States really had no vital interest at all in conflicts across the sea and could keep out of them if it wanted to.

In the American Creed the legal status of neutrality was enshrined as a moral principle and hence as a guide for all times and all circumstances. When President Wilson delivered his neutrality proclamation, he simply confirmed the popular belief that the current European conflict, like all the past conflicts, had arisen from purely European causes and would end in purely European consequences, and that the best thing for the United States to do was to conduct itself impartially and lend its moral prestige to the restoration of peace and sanity.

Yet, as Wilson well knew, neutrality was not simply an abstract principle, which a nation could follow without respect to the actions of other nations. Neutrality stood for a body of international law, more or less agreed upon, which not only imposed obligations but also granted rights. Therefore, even though America might remain faithful to its neutral obligations, if it insisted upon neutral rights which other nations were not prepared to grant, the very policy which was meant to preserve peace might draw the nation into war. From the first *Lusitania* note to the arming of American merchant vessels, the American people, as a whole, backed President Wilson in his insistence that Germany observe what the American government set forth as its just rights.

Although neutrality was posited upon America's indifference toward the fortunes of war, it was the fortunes of war, not America's legal impartiality, which determined the belligerents' willingness to observe American rights. However remote from the European conflict Americans might consider themselves, Europe could not ignore Americans, for the United States was a wealthy nation, determined to continue its commercial relations with the other side of the Atlantic, and the belligerents knew that the flow of American trade affected their very self-preservation. Under these circumstances neither belligerent stood to gain by observing a strict interpretation of American rights. Therefore, the ability of the United States to keep out of war depended, ultimately, upon the calculation which both belligerents made of the relative advantage of violating American rights as compared to the disadvantage of incurring American enmity. In the end, Germany preferred unrestricted submarine warfare to American neutrality, and, consequently, the United States was forced into the unenviable position of entering a foreign war to uphold a principle of national conduct that was based on the very premise that such a war could be of no vital interest.

In terms of national self-interest the issues of neutrality that faced America were simply: Is enforcing neutral rights rigidly against England worth the risk of a German victory? Is enforcing neutral rights rigidly against Germany worth the risk of a war with Germany? But to have framed the issue in this way would have meant the repudiation of neutrality and the surrender of national honor to expediency.

Moreover, few foresaw the unprecedented circumstances of submarine warfare. It was natural to try to apply conventional conceptions of neutrality at the outset. Yet once the United States had taken an official stand on a conventional interpretation, the American people proved that they preferred war to the dishonor of compromise.

Of course, the confusion in the public mind between wanting to keep out of war and demanding strict observance of American rights arose, basically, because Americans did not think in terms of alternatives. Their view of international relations was unclouded by such complexities. With innocent optimism they believed that they could eat their cake and have it too. Moreover, they lacked a central criterion, such as strategic interests, for discriminating among alternatives; and, being wedded to the illusion of isolation and omnipotence, they were contemptuous of the practical consequences of their national ideals and impulses. Without a realistic chart of the complex currents of national interests and power the nation was left to drift hazardously upon the turbulent waters of international politics, improvising its course as it went.

Americans might have been less emotionally entangled in the circumstances of the war if the issue of neutrality had been confined to the maintenance of legal rights; but Germany's submarine warfare violated America's sense of humanitarianism as well as its sense of honor. Having had little experience with the ravages of self-perservation upon international morality and having nurtured expectations of international morality scarcely warranted by the facts of world politics, the American people were appalled by the very existence of war and outraged by its breach of decency and humanity. Moreover, there was something peculiarly shocking and spectacular about sudden death by German torpedoes that was

lacking in the no less poignant tragedy of starvation by British blockade.

America's moral indignation over German submarine warfare was heightened by a general impression of German lawlessness and guilt, which began to take form with the invasion of Belgium. It was not only the invasion of that neutralized nation that aroused Americans but, just as much, Germany's official alibi on the grounds of expediency. Chancellor Bethmann-Hollweg's reference to the Belgian treaty as "just a scrap of paper" and Von Jagow's explanation that the safety of the Empire had rendered the violation of Belgian neutrality necessary were taken as standing indictments of Germany's Machiavellian contempt for international morality. In America the invasion of Belgium was pre-eminently a moral question; and yet the Germans excused themselves in terms of military necessity.

Germany's continual failure to provide a moral pretext for acts of expediency betrayed a basic ignorance of American psychology. The incidents of the war that really aroused American hostility toward Germany were incidents that violated the public's humanitarian sentiments: the destruction of Louvain and Rheims, reports of Belgian atrocities, the shooting of Nurse Edith Cavell, the deportation of Belgian and French labor. Ambassador Bernstorff was one of the few German officials who understood the extent to which Americans judged international affairs from the standpoint of emotional values and sentiments of justice and morality. But he could never get his superiors to understand this. In his book about his ambassadorship he complained, "In Germany there was no understanding for the curious mixture of political sagacity, commercial acumen, tenacity and sentimentality, which goes to make up the character of the American people."

Germany's violations of the laws of humanity were not, in themselves, sufficient provocation for American intervention, but the indignation which they aroused gave great moral assurance to America's strict interpretation of its neutral rights and made it possible to identify the nation's honor with the welfare of mankind. . . .

"Fear not the consequences when you know you are in the right." This would have made a fitting motto for America's intervention in World War I. On the part of some Americans, the motto would have represented bravado; on the part of others, altruism; for most it would simply have expressed a conditioned response to unforeseen circumstances. Few had calculated the effect of neutrality upon the nation's power position; fewer still were concerned with the expediency of intervention. Yet it was a dangerous oversimplification of the conditions of international politics to suppose that, in the long run, either universal ideals or the nation's self-interest could be achieved by ignoring these realities.

In the years after the war a great many Americans were embittered by the consequences of intervention and thoroughly convinced that intervention had been a terrible mistake. In retrospect, righteousness, honor, and the cause of world peace and democracy seemed inadequate motives for the grim sacrifices of war. The American mission, divorced from a conception of fundamental national self-interest, seemed to have been futile at best, false at worst; and the nation's scholars, journalists, and politicians set to work fixing the blame for intervention upon this group or that individual, as though to purge the nation of its guilt by indicting the selfishness, hypocrisy, or gullibility of a few.

To a certain extent the postwar mood was induced by the frustration of lofty expectations raised during the war. . . . Yet, even Utopia might not long have compensated the nation for participation in a foreign war if Utopia had seemed a thing apart from the national advantage, for only the most compelling objectives, those closest to fundamental self-interest, could have completely justified intervention in retrospect.

If the American people had been more altruistic, they would have gladly accepted the sacrifices of war as the legitimate price of an idealistic enterprise. If they had been more egoistic, they would not have required such high ideals from war. If Americans had been more realistic, they might have tempered both their egoistic and idealistic inclinations with the discipline of enlightened self-interest and a soberer estimate of the role of morality in international relations. Then America's relation to the European conflict might have seemed, in the aftermath of the war, more consistent with compelling national ends and motives.

This does not mean that American intervention was a mistake. Such a judgment implies that the alternative of nonintervention would have served American ideals and interests better; and this we can never know. It is, at least, possible that German submarines would have succeeded in crippling Great Britain's military effort and reducing the British Isles to a state of helplessness. There was always that risk. And it is almost certain, if the Treaty of Brest-Litovsk is any indication, that a peace settlement in which

Germany held the preponderance of power would have been infinitely more hostile to American ideals and interests than the severest critics of the Versailles Treaty claimed of that settlement. Allied victory guaranteed neither American ideals nor American interests, but at least it gave the nation the indispensable opportunity to achieve both ends through the establishment of a more peaceful and progressive international environment. Would nonintervention have been worth the risk of losing this opportunity?

If Woodrow Wilson erred, it was not because he led the United States into war but because he failed to do everything in his power to prepare the people to see their entrance into a foreign war as an act consistent with imperative principles of national self-interest, as well as with national ideals and sentiments. In fact, by stressing America's disinterestedness as a condition of her mission of bringing peace to the world, Wilson actually directed all the force of his leadership toward concealing what should have been the most compelling reason for American intervention.

If Americans, as a whole, supported intervention for insubstantial reasons, it was not because they were wrong in their idealism, their moral indignation, or their lively sense of national pride and honor; in the light of the international circumstances of 1914–17, there was justification for all these emotions. It was, rather, because they failed from the first to guide and restrain their aspirations and sentiments with a realistic view of national conduct and a prudent regard for the practical consequences of specific policies. For as a result of blind impulse and shortsightedness, their righteous indignation rested upon an uncertain legal case and an exaggerated ethical distinc-

tion between the belligerents, while their idealism, dissipated itself in a selfrighteous response to momentary passion. Americans, as a whole, were misguided in that they acted as though the complex task of reconciling the nation's self-interest with universal ideals could be simply and automatically achieved by satisfying certain emotional and temperamental proclivities in an unthinking response to the drift of events.

Armed intervention might well have been the wisest alternative from the long-run standpoint of American ideals and interests, but the great majority of the people did not choose war upon mature deliberation; they simply drifted into war, guided largely by impulses—some noble, some mean—with but a tenuous relation to broad and enduring national policy. Consequently, it is little wonder that the motives which led to war seemed inadequate in the perspective of peace, and that America's vaunted moral leadership revealed itself once more as the irresponsible outburst of a nation physically mature but emotionally and intellectually adolescent—a quick-tempered, good-hearted giant of a nation, moved by impulses it would later regret, undertaking commitments it would not fulfil, and never quite comprehending either the circumstances or the consequences of its erratic behavior.

Yet, lest the perspective of time distort our judgment of a different era, we shall do well to ponder the fact that each step that led to war was, in itself, consistent with the sentiments, beliefs, and policies which had evolved from America's previous experience in world politics; and that in the light of this experience each step was, at the time, a logical response to the unprecedented circumstances of an international conflict.

Suggestions for Further Reading

There are several good surveys of the literature on this subject which offer a useful starting point for additional reading. Among them are Richard W. Leopold, "The Problem of American Intervention, 1917: An Historical Retrospect," *World Politics*, II (April 1950), 405-425; Ernest R. May's pamphlet, *American Intervention: 1917 and 1941* (Washington, D.C., 1960) and his essay "Emergence to World Power" in John Higham (ed.), *The Reconstruction of American History* (New York, 1962); and Richard L. Watson, Jr., "Woodrow Wilson and his Interpreters, 1947–1957," *Mississippi Valley Historical Review*, LXIV (September 1957), 207-236.

The submarine thesis is most fully set forth in the works of Charles Seymour, notably in his narrative *American Diplomacy During the World War* (Baltimore, 1934) and in a slim volume of essays, *American Neutrality, 1914–1917* (New Haven, 1935). See especially the essay entitled "Woodrow Wilson and the Submarine." The thesis is ably seconded by Dexter Perkins, *America and Two Wars* (Boston, 1944). Still another expression of this view, by a former Wilson cabinet official, is Newton Baker, *Why We Went to War* (New York, 1936). Of the studies written in the post–World War II era the most impressive buttressing of Seymour's position is in Ernest R. May, *The World War and American Isolation, 1914–1917* (Cambridge, 1959) and in Arthur S. Link's contribution to the New American Nation series, *Woodrow Wilson and the Progressive Era, 1910–1917* (New York, 1954). Link's views on the reasons for American entry will presumably be elaborated in the later volumes of his massive biography of Wilson, the third and most recent volume of which, *Wilson: The Struggle for Neutrality, 1914–1915* (Princeton, 1960), goes only to fall 1915. Two recent specialized studies which by implication share the conclusion that the submarine was the chief cause of American involvement are Karl E. Birnbaum, *Peace Moves and U-Boat Warfare* (Stockholm, 1958), and Marion C. Siney, *The Allied Blockade of Germany, 1914–1916* (Ann Arbor, 1957).

Of Revisionist literature there is an abundance, and a good starting point would be the fairly complete but hostile survey of the field by D. F. Fleming, "Our Entry in the World War in 1917: The Revised Version," *Journal of Politics*, II (February 1940), 75–86. In addition to the works of Tansill, Peterson, Barnes, and Borchard and Lage that are represented in the present volume, there are two full-length books well worth reading. C. Harley Grattan's *Why We Fought* (New York, 1929) anticipates all the arguments that later occur in Revisionist writing, and Walter Millis' *Road to War: America, 1914–1917* (Boston, 1935), despite its sometimes sarcastic and belittling tone, is the most readable of all the narrative histories of the period. Volumes V and VI of Ray Stannard Baker's *Woodrow Wilson: Life and Letters* (Garden City, N.Y., 1935 and 1937), the earliest biography of the President to benefit from an examination of the Wilson papers, are also Revisionist in approach. A more legalistic study, in the pattern of Borchard and Lage, is Alice M. Morrissey, *The American Defense of Neutral Rights, 1914–1917* (Cambridge, Mass., 1939).

Close to Birdsall in its rejection of the Nye Committee's report and its affirmation of economic causation is Charles Beard, *The Devil Theory of War* (New York, 1936). Useful for two contemporary Congressional opponents of American entry whose views became touchstones for many Revisionist historians are Belle C. and Fola LaFollette, *Robert M. LaFollette* (2 vols.; New York, 1953) and George W. Norris, *Fighting Liberal* (New York, 1945).

The contents of British propaganda and the uses made of it are analyzed in James D. Squires, *British Propaganda at Home and in the United States from 1914–1917* (Cambridge, Mass., 1935) and Harold D. Laswell, *Propaganda Techniques in the World War* (New York, 1927). The single most influential piece of propaganda of the war, the Bryce Commission's *Report of the Committee on Alleged German Outrages,* was published in the *New York Times* of May 13, 1915.

Among the earliest to offer the view that the United States entered the war to maintain its security was a newspaperman, Forrest Davis, in *The Atlantic System: The Story of Anglo–American Control of the Seas* (New York, 1941). Walter Lippmann, with whom the thesis is chiefly identified, restated and refined the substance of his *Life* article in *United States Foreign Policy: Shield of the Republic* (Boston, 1943). Edward H. Buehrig's general support for that view is most fully stated in his *Woodrow Wilson and the Balance of Power* (Bloomington, Ind., 1955). A number of scholars have explicitly rejected the security thesis, among them Edward M. Earle, "A Half-Century of American Foreign Policy: Our Stake in Europe, 1898–1948," *Political Science Quarterly*, LXIV (June 1949), 168–188, and Thomas A. Bailey in the first chapter of his *Woodrow Wilson and the Lost Peace* (New York, 1944). But the most vigorous rejections have come from members of the Realist school, whose approach to foreign policy is most forcefully put in Hans Morgenthau, *In Defense of National Interest* (New York, 1951).

Because of Wilson's key role in the decision for war, the literature on him should be consulted. In addition to the older Baker and the unfinished Link multivolume biographies mentioned above, Arthur Walworth's sympathetic *Woodrow Wilson* (2 vols.; New York, 1958) is worth reading. Two short biographies which are sound and well written are John M. Blum, *Woodrow Wilson and the Politics of Morality* (Boston, 1956) and John A. Garraty, *Woodrow Wilson* (New York, 1956). Also useful for an insight into Wilson is Harley Notter, *The Origins of the Foreign Policy of Woodrow Wilson* (Baltimore, 1937). The centennial observance of Wilson's birth occasioned the publication of several pieces of a reflective sort, among the best of which are Arthur S. Link, *Wilson the Diplomatist* (Baltimore, 1957); Edward H. Buehrig (ed.), *Wilson's Foreign Policy in Perspective* (Bloomington, Ind., 1957); and Arthur P. Dudden (ed.), *Woodrow Wilson and the World Today* (Philadelphia, 1957). See especially William Langer's essays in the latter volume. The autumn 1956 and winter 1957 issues of *Confluence,* a periodical of the Harvard summer school, contain several thoughtful essays on Wilson and his foreign policy. Most of Wilson's important speeches and public documents can be found in Ray S. Baker and William E. Dodd (ed.), *The Public Papers of Woodrow Wilson* (6 vols.; New York, 1925–1927).

The published papers, memoirs, and biographies of Wilson's chief advisers should also be examined. Most important of the papers and memoirs are Charles Seymour (ed.), *The Intimate Papers of Colonel House* (4 vols.; Boston, 1926–1928); U.S. Department of State, *Papers Relating to the Foreign Relations of the United States, The Lansing Papers* (2 vols.; Washington, D.C., 1939–1940); and the posthumous *War Memoirs of Robert Lansing* (New York, 1935). Of the memoirs by Wilson's cabinet officials, only Secretary of Agriculture David Houston's *Eight Years with Wilson's Cabinet, 1913–1920* (New York, 1926) is moderately useful. The published recollections of Secretary of the Navy Daniels, Secretary of Commerce Redfield, and Secretary of the Treasury McAdoo are all disappointing on the subject of American entry. The memoirs of Wilson's colorful private secretary, Joseph P. Tumulty, *Woodrow Wilson as I Know Him* (New York, 1921), cannot be accepted at face value, but may be used with John M. Blum, *Joe Tumulty and the Wilson Era* (Boston, 1951). Biographies include Daniel Smith, *Robert Lansing and American Neutrality, 1914–1917* (Berkeley, Calif., 1958), and the older B. J. Hendrick, *The Life and Letters of Walter H. Page* (3 vols.; Garden City, N.Y., 1922–1925). None of the present biographies of William Jennings Bryan are especially good on his period as secretary of state.

There are several interesting memoirs by Englishmen and Germans which, if read with due caution, can be profitable. Chief among them are Sir Edward Grey, *Twenty-Five Years, 1892–1916* (2 vols.; New York, 1925), a book which supplied the Revisionists with much ammunition, and Johann H. von Bernstorff, *My Three Years in America* (New York, 1920), by the astute German ambassador. The memoirs of Arthur J. Balfour and David Lloyd George are also useful in parts, as is George M. Trevelyan's biography of the British Foreign Secretary, *Grey of Fallodon* (Boston, 1937). Stephen Gwynn (ed.), *The Letters and Friendships of Sir Cecil Spring Rice* (2 vols.; Boston, 1929), contains some interesting correspondence with Viscount Grey.